A Dedication

I take God the Father to be my God. 1. Thess 1:9

I take God the Son to be my Saviour Acts 5:31.

I take God the Holy Ghost to be my Sanctifier. 1 Pet 1:2

I take the Word of God to be my rule 2 Tim 3:16.17.

I take the people of God to be my people Ruth 1:16 17

I likewise dedicate my whole self to the Lord: Rom 14 7,8

And I do this deliberately Josh 24:15

Sincerely 2 Cor 1:12

Freely Psa. 110:3

And for ever Rom 8:35 39

FRANK.

THE RECORD of a

HAPPY LIFE.

THE RECORD

OF A

HAPPY LIFE:

BEING MEMORIALS OF

FRANKLIN WHITALL SMITH

A STUDENT OF

PRINCETON COLLEGE.

BY HIS MOTHER,

H. W. S.

ORIGINALLY PRINTED FOR PRIVATE CIRCULATION.

PHILADELPHIA:
J. B. LIPPINCOTT & CO.
1873.

Dedication.

For Frank's little brother and sisters, his cousins, and the circle of his loving friends, this book has been compiled, with many earnest prayers that they may learn from its pages the secret of the happy life they so well remember, and that they may make this secret their own.

It is essentially a boy's book, *and must be judged from a boy's standpoint. But if Frank's young life can but tell the "old, old story" in all its precious fulness, let none complain of the youth of the teacher, nor of the youthfulness of his ways.*

And may this history of the struggles, the failures and the victories of one whom they so loved, and who so earnestly desired day by day to be found walking in the Highway of Holiness, cheer and aid his young Christian friends, who like him are seeking to live up to the Bible standard, and who long to know that "victory which overcometh the world," and that "life which is hid with Christ in God!"

H. W. S.

THE RECORD

OF A

HAPPY LIFE.

CHAPTER I.

S I was sitting at the bedside of our boy on the afternoon he was taken sick, although no thought of danger had entered my mind, yet by one of those unaccountable impulses that sometimes lead the Christian into apparently strange things, for which afterwards he sees cause to be deeply thankful, I said to him, "Frank, this may be typhoid fever, and suppose thee should die; thee is not afraid, is thee?"

"Oh, no," he answered, very cheerfully, "not at all."

Pursuing my own train of thought as to the joys of entering upon the glorious eternity to be spent with Jesus, I added, after a moment, "It would be rather nice, would it not, to go?"

"Well, yes," he said, with a smile, "it *would;* only I would like to live a little longer to work for Jesus."

Ten days after that afternoon our Frank had left us to be with Jesus; and now we who are still on earth feel as if we would like, as far as possible, to fulfil the earnest longing of his heart, and to let him "work for Jesus." A sweet work, without any toil or weariness on his part, going on here on earth, while his head is safely pillowed on his Saviour's breast.

It is with this object, and to comfort our hearts with the sweet remembrances of his happy life, that the following account has been prepared, for those who knew and loved him. And his parents earnestly pray, that from among his loving circle of relations and friends, many bright stars may be added to his crown, through the instrumentality of this book.

Our boy was born in our house on Shoemakers' Lane, Germantown, August 12th, 1854. He was our second child; and three years of his little life were brightened by the sweet companionship of his sister Nelly, whose patronizing love and care for her "little Bud," as she called him, were a pretty sight to see. She seemed to consider herself responsible for his good behavior on all occasions, and evidently felt as if everything she learned was valuable only as she could teach it to him. One little scene, when he was just three years old, is too sweet to be forgotten. We were spending the summer at grandpa Whitall's house at Atlantic City. I had put the two children to bed one evening, and had left the room, when, hearing their voices, I stopped outside to listen. I heard Nelly say, "Franky, does thee know that Heavenly Father don't hear thee when thee prays, unless thee thinks about what thee is saying?"

"Don't he?" asked Frank, wonderingly.

"No indeed," answered Nelly; "and thee ought to think how good He is, and how He loves us, and gives us good things, while the poor little beggars go from door to door." Then she continued, "Franky, shall I tell thee a story about praying? Once there was a little boy, and his mother was very poor and had no bread, and he said, 'Mother, I'll get some bread.' And he went in a corner and kneeled down and prayed, 'Please, Heavenly Father, give us some bread.' And he thought about what he was saying, Franky, and Heavenly Father heard him, and put a great big basket full in a good woman's heart, and she took it to the poor people, and they had plenty to eat. So thee sees, Franky," she moralized, "we must always think about what we say."

Her exhortations seemed to be understood by little Frank, and he asked, "Does thee think about thine?"

"Oh, yes," replied Nelly, "always. Let me show thee." And she repeated her little prayer very solemnly, saying, at the end, "There, Franky, I thought about that."

Frank's sense of condemnation for his own formal prayer was by this time thoroughly aroused, and he called out at the top of his voice, "Mamma, mamma, come back; I want to say my prayer over again, and think about it."

And his little thoughtful voice and manner, as he repeated his childish requests, showed how effectual the lesson had been.

What such a companionship would have been to him as he grew up, we cannot tell; for, a few months after this time, on Christmas morning, 1857, our darling Nelly was taken home to heaven, at the age of five years and five months; and as no more children were added to the family for eight years, Frank was for all that time an only child. He was also the oldest grandchild in the families of both his grandpa Smith and grandpa Whitall, and was an especial joy and delight, petted by all around him.

A very sweet, fascinating little fellow he was, full of gentle and generous impulses, and developing daily many winning little traits. But he had also a naturally obstinate, wilful temper, and until he was between four and five years of age, the peculiar circumstances by which he was surrounded made him quite naughty at times; and his fits of loud crying, followed by long sullen spells, were very much dreaded by his mother and aunties.

About this age, however, a great change took place in him. His father and I, who had long been seeking the truth, were both brought on the same day, during the summer of 1858, to a knowledge of the Lord Jesus Christ as our all-sufficient Saviour, bearing our sins in His own body on the tree; and by faith in Him were "born again" into the family of God. Almost at once we began to wonder whether Frank could understand this blessed gospel. He seemed too young. We thought it almost useless to try; and yet the news of salvation was too good to be kept from our child, and we told him as simply as possible the story of Jesus and His love. To our amazement, — so ignorant were we then of the meaning of those words of our Lord, "Suffer little children to come unto me, and forbid them not, for of such is the kingdom of heaven,"—Frank seemed to understand. The blessed Holy Spirit carried home the truth to his little heart. His soul was brought under a real conviction of his sinfulness and his need of a Saviour, and in his gentle childish way, easily and simply, he too believed and was born again.

Among my old papers I find the following account, written at the time, and as I have read it over and over since his death, every scene it describes comes up before me with vivid intensity.

"Our little boy, only four years old, has been converted this past winter. We had never taught him anything about trusting Jesus, because we did not know it ourselves. And we had contented ourselves with general instructions about God as a Father in heaven, and about His moral law as the rule of life. And even after we had learned the truth for ourselves, it seemed to us for a while that it was impossible for one so young to understand anything about it. But having heard the story of a little girl who had been saved, our eyes were opened to the fact that even little children could come to Jesus and find forgiveness. And with earnest prayer that the truth as it is in Jesus might be blessed to our child, we began to tell him the blessed story. He listened to it wonderingly and gladly. The Holy Spirit made him feel himself to be a sinner needing a Saviour, and at once he seemed to open his gentle heart to admit the dear Lord who was knocking for entrance.

"The fruits of the Spirit at once began to show themselves in him very manifestly. He loves to talk of Jesus, and to hear stories about Him, and repeats over and over again, 'Mamma, I love Heavenly Jesus best of all.' He has become gentle and yielding, and full of love, even his little face shining often with a real heavenly light, and all his old sullen tempers seem to have disappeared almost entirely. This change is so striking that even our casual visitors cannot but notice it, for he was formerly one of the most obstinate and difficult of children, so that we at times almost despaired of conquering him. Now, when he is tempted to be naughty, he runs away by himself for a little while, and then comes back with a bright smile on his face, and in gentle tones makes a pleasant remark, watching eagerly to see how it will be received. Several times when this has occurred I have said, 'Frank, did thee ask Heavenly Jesus to send the good angel into thy heart?' and he has answered, 'Yes, mamma, I said it in my heart, and right away He heard me and sent the good angel to drive the naughty one away.' But sometimes his answer has been, 'No, mamma, I did not ask Him, for He sent it right in Himself, quick before I had time to ask.'

"He loves to talk about our spirits going up to heaven, and seems fully to realize that the spirit is the part of us that loves and trusts Jesus, and wants to please Him. Once when we had been talking together on these things, his face lighted up with a lovely, enthusiastic little smile, and he said, 'Oh, mamma, I do love Heavenly Jesus so! If He was standing here by me, I would wipe my mouth right clean, and would kiss and hug Him all the time.' Then, after a pause, he added, 'and, mamma, I will save ever so many hugs on my hands to give Him when we go up to meet Him in the clouds.'

"The darling child seems to have no fear of death, but rather to desire it, and sometimes he will say in the morning, 'Oh, mamma, maybe it will be Heavenly Father's time for me to go up to Heaven to-day, and then I will be *so* glad.'

"A short time after his conversion, he taught me a lesson I shall never forget. I had been teaching him to pray every evening—'O Lord Jesus, please give me a new heart that will love thee.' He was for a while very earnest in praying, saying it two or three times in the evening, and asking us to remind him to say it in the morning; and it was very sweet to see him,—his little hands clasped, and his eyes closed, pausing reverently a moment in silence, and then saying the few simple words so confidently, as though sure of a speedy answer. But one night, after I had read his usual little story to him, and had tucked him up comfortably in bed, as I leaned over him to listen to his last prayer, he said, 'Mamma, I want to pray, but I don't know what to pray for.' 'Why not say thy usual prayer for a new heart?' I asked. 'Oh, mamma,' he answered, 'I *can't* say that any more, for I did ask Heavenly Jesus for a new heart, and He gave it me, and I have got it now. And besides,' he added, 'I know it is a soft heart, for it loves Heavenly Jesus so much. So now, mamma, what *shall* I pray for?' I suggested that he should ask to be so very good that everybody would see it, and it would teach them to love Jesus too. 'Oh, but,' he replied, 'I am too little to be a preacher.' 'No,' was my answer, 'thee is not.' And then I told him of some very little children who had trusted Jesus, and had talked to others about Him, and had been the means, some of them, of bringing even men and women to believe in Him and love Him. Frank listened with deep interest, and said at last, 'Well, mamma, *I* want to preach to the soldiers; and if papa will take me to their house, I will say, Do you love Jesus? and if they say, No, I will tell them to do it, and then they will. So, mamma, I will pray for that.' And with clasped hands, and an earnest little face, he said, 'Please, dear Heavenly Jesus, make me *so* good that everybody will know that I love thee; and please let me preach to the soldiers, and tell them to love thee, and to throw their guns away.'

"Since then, something like this has been his nightly prayer; and he often adds, with beseeching earnestness, 'Please, never, never, never let me do anything naughty any more!'"

How well I remember it all. My incredulity as to the possibility of so young a child being converted, and my slowness in believing in the reality of it, even after I saw daily so many proofs. But looking back now over the fourteen years that followed, I see how wonderfully real and true it all was, and what a radical change did at this period take place in our boy. From that time I have no recollection of anything in him ever needing punishment, scarcely of anything calling for reproof. And yet his life was so thoroughly natural and boyish, that while it was passing it had no sense of strained piety, such as we have been too apt to associate with the idea of children converted young. From first to last he was a joyous, happy, natural boy, ready to enter into all sorts of innocent fun, rejoicing in every manly sport, fond of gunning, sailing, climbing, swimming, and base-ball and cricket; and always the foremost to lead in any adventurous expedition.

His religion did not deprive him of happiness, but increased it tenfold. He could afford to be natural, because having been made a partaker of the Divine Nature through faith in Christ, it became to a great degree natural to him to do right. Relieved from all anxiety about his salvation, he was free of heart to throw himself into every innocent pursuit or pleasure that came to him; and the result has been a life which it is a perfect delight to contemplate, so unstained seemed its last fourteen years to our sight with any care, or sorrow, or sin. He said himself, in the last conversation he had with his darling cousin Minnie, to whom he confided everything, that in looking back over his life he believed he had always had everything he wanted, and had done just what he pleased. And this was very much the case. I can scarcely remember his ever expressing a wish that we found it necessary to deny; and we were able, for many years before his death, to grant him almost the entire control of his actions in every respect. It was because his heart was right with God, that this could be. And it is a beautiful exemplification of what the religion of Jesus was intended to do for us, taking effect first upon the inward life, and then producing its results naturally, and therefore easily, upon the outward actions. Being "born again" into the family of God, and knowing it, it was characteristic of his new nature to desire, above everything else, to live and walk as became such a position, and such a relationship.

What a glorious proof such a life is, that the Lord Jesus Christ came to make us happy, and to give us liberty, if only we so understood His gospel as to apprehend that ourselves, for which we are apprehended of Him.

Only a month or two before his death, I said to Frank, on the occasion of some especial pleasure he had been enjoying, "Frank, it does seem as if all the good times come to thee." And then added, "I do believe it is just because thee has given thyself to Jesus, and trusts Him with everything, and so He manages for thee to have a real happy time all the while." He laughed in his quiet way, and said, "I really think it must be so, for I certainly do seem to have the best time of any one I know."

Surely his life has been throughout an illustration of the truth, that if we seek *first* the kingdom of God and His righteousness, all things needful shall be added unto us; and that no good thing will God withhold from them that walk uprightly.

After Frank's conversion, his childhood flowed on very happily, his little heart learning easily the lessons of faith, and acquiring very quickly the blessed habit of going to Jesus with all his childish needs and childish troubles. His confidence in prayer often amazed us. I remember very well one occasion when he was about seven years old. We were passing the summer in a little cottage on his grandpa

Smith's place on Shoemakers' Lane, Germantown. Frank had spent his little stock of money for a certain kind of toys which were all the fashion among the boys at that time; and I felt as if a due sense of economy and propriety forbade him having any more. So, as I handed him the last of the toys, I said, "Frank, this is all, remember. When this is gone, thee cannot have any more." He made no reply, and I thought the matter was ended. Shortly after I went up the main street to do some errands, and on my way home passed a store where these toys were for sale. I noticed them at first, without any thought of Frank, but after having passed by some distance, I began to feel as if I must go back and buy the little fellow some more. The feeling increased so much, and made me so uncomfortable, that at last I walked back several squares and made the purchase. When I reached the house, Frank came running out to the gate to meet me, and said, in the most confident little way possible, "Well, mamma, where are my toys?" "Why, Frank," said I, quite surprised, "don't thee remember that I told thee, thee could not have any more?" "Oh, yes," he answered, "but then I asked Jesus to tell thee to bring me some, and I *know* thee has got them."

Another time, while still living in this cottage, Frank was dangerously sick with the measles, and was utterly unable to retain a drop of water on his stomach, yet he was consumed with thirst. One evening, after a day of great suffering, he said to me just at nightfall, "Mamma, I want thee to come here and pray that I may go to sleep, and sleep sound all night, and wake up to-morrow morning with my stomach well, so that I can drink." I rather hesitated, feeling that there was no hope of his prayer being answered, but was at once checked for my want of faith, and said, "I will, Frank, if thee has faith. Can thee believe that God will do it?" "Oh, yes," he answered, "I am sure He will; so just pray." I accordingly kneeled beside his bed, and asked for the things he wanted. He then fixed himself for sleep, and said, "Now, mamma, tell Ellen to get up early in the morning and go down to Mr. Thompson's spring, and bring up a big pitcher of water, and set it by my door with two tumblers, so as to be all ready when I wake up." And then he quietly went off to sleep. I obeyed his injunctions to the letter, feeling thoroughly stirred up by the child's faith, and yet so doubtful as to the result that I resolved in myself never to mention the subject of water again until he did. Need I say, however, that according to his faith it was unto him? Frank slept delightfully, waked up at daylight, and called for his water. It was all waiting for him just as he had ordered, and he sat up in bed and drank two full tumblers with the most intense enjoyment; and not an uncomfortable feeling followed. Verily God hath hidden these things from the wise and prudent, and hath revealed them unto babes.

Many similar instances I could relate, but these are sufficient. This habit of confiding prayer was never lost, and to it, no doubt, was owing much of the happy even tenor of his young life. Before the years had come when doubts are so apt to harass the soul, Frank had learned too deeply ever to unlearn it, the blessed truth that God means what He says when He tells us to ask and we shall receive, and when He urges us to be careful for *nothing*, but in *everything* to make our requests known unto Him. He realized that all things, both great and small, were included in the two words *nothing* and *everything;* and as a consequence his life was largely filled with that peace which is declared to be the portion of those who know this secret.

CHAPTER II.

WHEN Frank was about five years old, a dear friend of his father's died, leaving a widow with four little children. We took one of them home with us for a visit, to relieve the delicate mother for a time of some of her numerous cares, a little girl named Sally, of just about Frank's age. She proved to be a dear good little girl and nice company for Frank, and after her mother's death, which occurred within a year or two of her father's, we concluded to keep her altogether, and she grew up with our boy, a bright pleasant companion for him, adding very much to the pleasures of his life.

At about the age of eight years, a very grave danger threatened Frank, and he was committed to the Lord in a most especial manner. A very wicked man, whom we had been obliged to thwart in some of his wicked purposes in reference to a child in the —— ——— of which institution we were at the time managers, wrote us a most abusive threatening letter. In it he declared his intention of taking his revenge on us through our son, by leading him into wickedness and making him as bad as himself. As I read the letter, my heart sank within me. I thought of the thousand ways in which such a threat could be fulfilled, and how powerless we were to prevent it. I was afraid to have my boy out of my sight for a moment, and felt as if we would have to move out of Philadelphia, away to the ends of the earth, anywhere to get out of the reach of this wicked man. But then I realized that even this might not be effectual; and in my despair I fled to the Lord for help. At once there came to me, as a voice from heaven, that blessed promise — "The angel of the Lord encampeth round about them that fear Him, and delivereth them;" with the assurance that so would the angels encamp around our boy and deliver him from this and every danger. My heart leapt up in happy confidence, as I gave him at once into this blessed guardianship; every fear vanished; and as I saw him leave the house for school the next morning, I could almost see the cohorts of angels surrounding him on every side. I believe I never again feared any danger for him, so sure was I that the Lord was his defence and his shield on every hand. Who can doubt that God did then and there, according to His word, take the charge of the child thus committed to Him, in an especial manner; and that from henceforth He encamped round about him continually, leading him safely through all the dangers of life, and landing him now at last unharmed in his heavenly home?

At the age of ten years Frank had a fresh awakening in his religious life, and, under the influence of some meetings he was attending, for the first time made a public confession of his faith in Christ. He grew up a noble, pure boy, recoiling from intimacies with other boys whom he found to be persisting in wrong courses; and breaking off of his own accord two or three friendships, begun when he was very young, because he found his friends were developing wrong propensities. About one or two of these I remonstrated, seeing only the fair exterior of his childhood's friends; but he said, with a look of such dignified purity, "Mother, if thee *knew* those boys, thee would be only thankful that I cannot like them."

Just about this age of ten years a great joy came to Frank. His little sister Mary was added to the family, and she was destined to be to him a source of untold delight during the eight years they were together, and to receive from him the tenderest and sweetest love and care that ever a big brother gave to a little sister. His ways with her were lovely, a perfect combination of brother, and father, and playmate all in one; and it was a great joy to us to see them together. As a little baby, Mariechen, as her German nurse called her, soon learned to read the story of love out of her brother's eyes, and would go to him from any one, even her mother. And as she grew older, their talks and plays together were among her chiefest delights. He called her "Rogey-pogey," because of her mischief, and she called him "Long-lank," because he was so tall; and the very words, as I write them, bring up visions of many a merry ride and walk, and evening romp. After Frank left home for college, they kept up quite a correspondence, and a letter from "Bubba" was always hailed with a shout of joy. One of his letters I will insert as a record of their happy intercourse.

"HAV. COLL. 3mo. 19, 1871.

"MY OWN DARLING LITTLE SISTER:

"As I was walking up to my desk the other day, somebody said, 'Frank, there is a little three-cornered letter in thy desk for thee.' And then I thought, 'Who can have written me a letter in a three-cornered envelope?' But when I saw mother's handwriting on it, and a letter 'M.' on the back, then I knew a young one they call Mary Whitall Smith had sent it. And then I tried to think how much I loved that young 'un, but I could n't remember, it was *so* much. Then I opened the letter and read it, and now I am answering it. What did thee draw that picture for, thee scamp? Look out for a spanking when I come home! Thee knows it don't look like me. Does thee know thee called me Tumblebug? What can I do to punish thee? Something awful, I guess.

"Who taught thee to write so well? I did n't know I had a sister who was such a good writer. Thee can write almost as well as I can.

". . . But, thee sweet one, I must stop. With ever so much love, I remain thy very affectionate 'bubba,' FRANK!"

To this sister, as well as to the three younger children born afterwards, the loss of such an older brother is greater than we can express. But we must believe that He who gave, and who has taken away, will Himself be to them more than even the tenderest brother.

In the fall of the year 1864, Frank's father took

charge of the glass factories at Millville, New Jersey, belonging to the firm of Whitall, Tatum & Co., of which he had become a member. And we moved there, taking up our abode in the Mansion House situated in the factory grounds, on a high bluff overlooking the Maurice River, and surrounded by old oak-trees. It was in this free country life that Frank developed the fondness for manly pursuits, which added so much to his pleasures and to the force of his character. We felt so unwilling to send him to boarding-school, that we had tutors for him at home for three years, and they largely made up to him for his isolation from other companionship, joining in his riding and gunning, and sailing and skating, and rousing him to energy and manliness. The wild nature of the country around Millville afforded many opportunities for hunting and exploring expeditions; and I was continually being called on to put up lunches overnight, for a start on some such excursion before the dawn of the next day.

I love to think of our boy at this time, in his free joyous country life, and I am so glad we lavished upon him every innocent gratification that could make his life brighter. I remember the great epoch when he became the owner of a gun. A rash indulgence I thought it, but could not find it in my heart to make a single objection, when I found his father was willing, and saw how the boy's heart was set upon it. And he has often told us since that nothing ever gave him such exquisite pleasure as the arrival of that gun, with its brown paper wrappings and powdery smell.

I remember a sweet little incident connected with

this gun which I must insert here, because it so beautifully illustrates the effect of grace on the heart. Frank's father never hesitated to let his boy know when he was gratified with his conduct, and one day, soon after the arrival of the gun, he said to him, on the occasion of some fresh instance of obedience:

"Frank, I want thee to know how I appreciate thy ready instantaneous obedience to my wishes, and how fully thy father's love is satisfied with his son."

Dear Frank smiled and said, "Has thee noticed any difference since thee gave me that gun, father?"

"No," was the reply; "thee has always been so good that I do not know that I have noticed any especial change."

"Well," said Frank, "I think there has been some, anyhow, for I felt as if thee must love me so much to give me that gun, that I have wanted more than ever since then, to do just everything thee wishes."

It is thus grace always acts on a true heart; and the lesson which Frank learned in the tender love of his earthly father, was beautifully repeated when he came fully to understand the love of his Heavenly Father.

It never seemed to us that religion was intended to make a boy unnatural, or to turn him into a premature old man. And we encouraged his amusements as heartily as we did his religion, sure that his Father in heaven had given him richly all things to enjoy, and that we were the appointed channels through which these good things were to be handed forth to him. Through his whole life this was our feeling; and it is unspeakably comforting now, in looking back, to remember that he always had our hearty sympathy and help in every project of pleasure he proposed. It was very seldom that we found any need of objecting to any of his wishes, but on the few occasions when this did occur, he was so sure of our earnest desire always to gratify him where it was possible, that he found no difficulty in yielding. And there never was a shade upon the most perfect openness and freedom of our mutual intercourse. Frank knew all of our secrets, and we knew his, and I am sure no father and son ever more thoroughly delighted in each other than did our boy and his father.

In the spring of 1866, when Frank was twelve years old, some of his cousins and friends of about his own age came down to Millville to spend the Easter holidays. They were a happy young party, and made the house, and woods, and river ring again with their joyous merriment. Among other things they formed a society called the "S. S. S.," which was from that time the centre of a great deal of interest to all its members, and the source of much happiness to our boy.

Its object was to bear a protest against the tendency of the age towards making boys and girls into premature young ladies and gentlemen, and for the promotion of healthy, hearty, youthful fun. They had a regular Constitution, with rules and regulations, some of which were very amusing, and yet perhaps truly sensible also. Article I. read as follows:

"Be it enacted, that we, the members of this society, do one and all pledge ourselves to unite together in an unbroken phalanx to resist the fearful assaults being made upon 'fun' in the present age of the world."

ARTICLE II. "Be it enacted, that each member of this society be required to plan and carry out all sorts and manner of fun, upon every possible occasion, and to join in it wherever it may be going on. Also to laugh, shout, climb, race, leap, and tumble whenever moved thereto."

ARTICLE III. "Be it enacted, that our members, when together, shall only wear such garments as shall be able to stand the wear and tear of fun; garments that can scale rocks, wade streams, climb trees, walk fences, and run races. Further, be it enacted, that our garments shall never be in the height of the fashion."

ARTICLE VIII. "Be it enacted, that fun, according to our meaning of the word, includes the play of the intellect, as well as the play of the body; that a race of wits is as legitimate as a race of feet, or a leap of the fancy as a leap over fences, and that to climb means as well to scale the hills of knowledge as the hills of nature. Be it enacted, therefore, that we keep each other stirred up to all sorts of mental activity, as well as bodily; and that to further this, debates, essays, epistles, and skirmishes of the wits generally, shall be continually carried on among us, by letter and otherwise."

ARTICLE IX. "Be it enacted, that we have as frequent meetings as possible, and that we always meet, whenever practicable, at 'Liberty Hall,' kept by

R. P. & H. W. S., and that between our meetings we keep up a vigorous correspondence."

ARTICLE X. "Be it enacted, finally, that we never grow old in feeling ourselves, nor ever permit any one else to do so."

The hearty innocent associations and interests of this S. S. S. Society, we felt to be very valuable to our boy; and we are sure they contributed not a little to the healthy development of his character, preserving him in a large measure from the sentimental unreality of the age, and inciting him to all that was truly natural and manly.

In the fall of 1867, Frank's cousin, Whitall Nicholson, the next to him in age of the large family of grandpa Whitall's grandchildren, came to Millville to spend the winter, studying and playing with Frank. It was a merry, happy winter, filled with quite as much play as study, and one that we all enjoyed very much. I find in one of my old letters to Whitall's mother the following reference to it:—"The two boys are so happy together that it is a pleasure to have them about. Their rifles have come, and they are full of excitement about them, cleaning, and greasing, and getting the very blackest hands that ever adorned the ends of any boy's arms. They have a great deal of fun modelling the clay used for the glass pots into mock battles, and Whitall's figures are really capital. They do this in the evening, while Mr. F. or I read to them out of 'Queens of England.' They are making scrap books too. And their workshop is always a resource for rainy days; and altogether, they are a busy and happy pair of chaps."

CHAPTER III.

DURING all this time at Millville, Frank was surrounded with very precious religious influences, both from the circle of friends who visited us, and from the natural flow of happy Christian life and conversation which was the atmosphere of our household. It was an inestimable blessing to him, that the truth set before him was the pure gospel of Jesus Christ, unmixed with the commandments or traditions of men. It had been the privilege of his parents, after many years of seeking, to be brought out clearly into the full light of the gospel of grace; and from the moment when our boy had started to walk in the heavenly pathway, at the age of four years, we had endeavored carefully to guard him from the many errors that so often obscure the truth as it is in Jesus.

Frank was taught that the Lord Jesus Christ was the Lamb of God that taketh away the sin of the world, and that in His atoning death on the cross He did bear our sins in His own body, and did take upon Himself the stripes that were our due. He was taught that by means of this sin-bearing, God had reconciled the world unto Himself, and that He no longer imputed their trespasses unto them; and he understood the gospel to be a message of glad tidings to sinners, telling them the wondrous fact that their iniquities had been taken off of them, and laid upon the Lord Jesus Christ, and that God was reconciled to them by the death of his Son. Thus understanding the gospel, it was easy for Frank to see, that the only thing left for him to do in the matter was to believe this good news, and through believing to find eternal life. He was taught that his own part in the work of salvation was simply to believe, and that then the blessed Holy Spirit would never fail to do His accompanying work of creating within him a new heart and a right spirit. "He that believeth hath everlasting life," the believing only being our part, the giving of eternal life being the work of God, always accompanying our believing. Thus the plan of salvation was not hidden from Frank by any system of works. He was taught that good works must follow, and not precede, the new birth; that they were the results of this new birth, and not the cause of it. And he learned thoroughly the blessed truth, that the Christian life ought to *begin* with the knowledge of the forgiveness of sins, instead of this knowledge being attained only at the end of a long course of faithful obedience and service.

It was a happy faith that our boy was taught, and the results were to be seen in a life, even then almost blameless, and a confiding trust in His Saviour that shed a brightness over all his pursuits and pleasures.

Such was Frank, during our life at Millville. But after all, his religion was not an *active* religion. It made him good, and obedient, and dependable, but it did not make him zealous in the Lord's work, nor enable him to bear any open or public testimony to his Master. He was naturally exceedingly reserved, and it seemed as if it was almost an impossibility for him to open his mouth to confess the Lord Jesus before men. We felt that more was needed before he would be the earnest working Christian we longed to see him, but the way to supply this need we could not yet see. God, however, had His messengers all ready, who were to bring to our house the glad tidings of a sufficiency to be found in the Lord Jesus, not only for our future salvation, but for our utmost present needs as well. They were to supply the missing link in our knowledge of the gospel. We had, as I have shown, learned thoroughly the blessed truth of justification by faith, and rejoiced in it with great joy. But here we had stopped. The equally blessed twin truth of sanctification by faith had not yet been revealed to us. And we had long been conscious that for ourselves, as well as for Frank, there was a need of far more spiritual power than we yet possessed, and for a secret of victory over temptation, that would enable us always to triumph, where as yet we suffered many and sorrowful defeats.

And at last the time came. In the fall of the year 1866, there came as Tutor to Frank, a young Baptist theological student. He had not been long in our house, before we discovered that he had a secret of continual victory and abiding rest of which we were ignorant. After watching him for many months, continually impressed with the wonderful purity and devotedness of his life, we began to ask him about it. And he told us that his simple secret was faith.

He trusted, and Jesus delivered. He laid the care of his life, moment by moment, on the Lord, and the Lord took it, and made his life moment by moment what He would have it to be. It was a wonderful revelation. At the same time, some of the workmen in our factory, having also come into the experience of this life of faith, began to come to our house to talk about it; and we all attended, Frank and all, a little evening meeting, held for the consideration and promotion of this truth. The result was at last, that Frank's father and myself were brought out into a clear knowledge of the truth of sanctification by faith, and realized in the wondrous peace, and victory, and liberty of this new life, that we had known before only half the gospel. Our dear boy also was thoroughly aroused, and began then dimly to understand the truth which a year or two later was to be so beautifully developed in his experience, and was to make him so early ripe for his heavenly home.

The following letter, written to this Tutor, in the spring of 1868, will show the work of the Spirit in his heart, and his felt and acknowledged needs.

"MILLVILLE, N. J., March 1st, 1868.

"DEAR MR. F.:

"I promised I would write to you, a good while ago, but I have never kept my promise, so I will do so now. Last evening we went to the Methodist holiness experience meeting, where almost every body spoke. I felt led to speak, but Satan said 'Nobody wants to hear *you;* you had better keep your seat. Just think how awful it would be for you to stand up and face everybody there; you would feel terribly.' And he conquered. But, Mr. F., I want you to pray for me, that I may be able to take up the cross for my dear Saviour, who has done so much for me. Mr. F., we have a dear Saviour; I am sure I don't half appreciate what He has done for me, but I am doing so more and more.

"Mr. McAfee and I have cleaned out the boat-house, and covered the bottom with sand; we have dug out the channel to the river, and put up a fence on one side. Since the snow we have been coasting down the hill to the boat-house.

"Last Saturday evening, that is a week from yesterday, after the holiness meeting, which was a very nice one, when I was in bed, I thought somehow this way—If these Methodists have such a blessing, why should not I? Why, no reason at all. So I just prayed that I might have the peace of God shed abroad in my heart; and I had it, and it made me so happy! And oh, Mr. F., I want you to pray that I may be all the time growing in grace.

"We are all well, as I hope you are. Little Bay told us this morning she was never going to marry!

"Good-bye, from your loving brother in the Lord,

"F. W. Smith."

The blessed Spirit had begun thus early to open our dear boy's eyes to the wonderful privileges of the higher Christian life; but it was not until two years later, in the spring of 1870, that his soul was brought into the full experience of it.

Among his old papers, we have come across

a few leaves of a journal kept about this time, which contains the following entries:

"FIRST-MO. 18th, 1868.

"I am a boy, a little over thirteen years of age, with a kind, loving father and mother. But better than this, I have a much kinder and much more loving Heavenly Father, who gave His only-begotten Son to die for me, and save me from eternal destruction. I became a Christian somewhat over nine years ago, but I have been a very naughty one ever since. I have disobeyed my earthly parents, but far worse, I have disobeyed my Heavenly Father. But, thank God, I have come out of that reign of sin, by believing that He has not only forgiven me my sins, but also destroyed the body of sin in me. So long as I believe this, I am happy; but the moment I stop clinging to Him, I am overwhelmed with sin, and am miserable until I again return.

"My lot is indeed a happy one. I have a dear, kind, loving father, who would do anything almost to please me; a dear, kind, loving mother, who sympathizes with me in all my joys and sorrows, and who advises me in all my perplexities; a sweet sister Mary, four years old, whom I love with all my heart, and who returns my love again; a baby sister Alice, six months old; a little brother Logan, two years old, and an adopted sister, who is about my own age."

"FIRST-MO. 19th.

"This afternoon I went skating with my tutor, and learned how to cut a circle backwards for the first time. In the evening heard Mr. Coleman preach a splendid sermon on sanctification, from Matt. i. 21."

"FIRST-MO. 24th.

"Warm again; skating soft. Began Irving's Life of Washington to-day, rather reluctantly, but at father's request, and found it very interesting indeed."

"FIRST-MO. 25th.

"Cold again, and splendid skating. I can roll forwards, cut a circle backwards and forwards, spread the eagle, skate backwards and forwards,—and tumble down!"

"FIRST-MO. 26th.

"To-day is First-day. I used to think it a great bore for First-day to come, but now I enjoy it, though not as much as I ought to. Sorted father's tracts for him."

"SECOND-MO. 6th.

"No skating to-day, but we took a splendid sail this afternoon. It was terrible hard rowing back. Took a fine sleigh-ride this evening by moonlight. (Young ladies were wanted to complete the fun.)"

"SECOND-MO. 20th.

"Had a splendid sail this afternoon, rowing down the river and sailing back. This morning three men were converted in our factory; and this evening another one was brought to know Christ as his Redeemer. Went to a Methodist Experience meeting, the best I have ever been to."

Thus his life passed happily along, both inwardly and outwardly, while many circumstances were conspiring in the Providence of God to form his character, and give him the perfect dependableness which was afterwards so remarkable in him.

We had very strong convictions as to the importance of a late education, as giving time for the solid development of the mental powers, and avoiding the great danger of any overstrain of mind and body. We concluded, therefore, in the fall of 1868, to intermit a year of study, and to let him go into the counting-room of the firm in Philadelphia, under the care of his uncle, James Whitall, for the winter. It was a great trial to let him go away from home, and seemed like somewhat of an experiment to send a petted home boy, who had hardly done anything but play all his life-long, into a counting-room with trained clerks, where steady work would be expected from him. But we believed the discipline would be invaluable to him; and we had confidence in our boy. We sent him away with many prayers, and with a confiding trust that the Lord, to whose care we committed him, would guard him from every danger. He made his home at his dear grandpa Smith's, in Germantown, and in the tender love and care of his grandpa and grandma, and his darling "aunty Lill," he was made as happy almost as if he had been at home. A very tender tie existed between Frank and this aunt. From his earliest babyhood she had been delighted to have him much with her; and her self-sacrificing love was repaid with an affection both filial and brotherly. I always felt happy about him when he was under her care, knowing that every need of his heart, and mind, and body also, would all be most lovingly and judiciously provided for.

Under this happy guardianship, Frank passed the winter, more than fulfilling all our expectations, and even our hopes, in regard to his counting-house duties. From every one in any way connected with the business, there came at the time, and has come since, one unvarying testimony as to his uniform faithfulness in the discharge of his duties, and his lovely, gentlemanly deportment to all around him. To our hearts it was sweetest music, to hear such praises of our absent boy.

In the few leaves left of his Diary, we find the following reference to this change:

"September 7th, 1868.

"To-day I began my work at the store in Philadelphia, away from home, and almost all religious influences. Oh! how I pray that I may be kept ever near to my precious Jesus. In the evening I went to Germantown, and received a hearty welcome at Ivy Lodge, and a real nice room all to myself."

Again, under date of First-mo. 23d, 1869, he wrote:

"I do not often write anything connected in this book, but every now and then I like to jot down what interests me most. At present it is that our whole family is to move up to Philadelphia to live. On Christmas I was home and went deer-hunting, but shot nothing.

"During the last week I have been attending lectures on Geology. Very interesting.

"As the days move on, I am afraid I am not progressing much in the kingdom of God. I pray constantly, and yet I cannot put my full trust in Christ. I do not know why, though. It is not because He would betray my trust; oh, no! for I know He could not do that. I do trust Him in some measure, but I have not the blessing of a clean conscience. So far as I do trust Him though, He does deliver me."

He came home every week during the winter, so that we did not receive many letters from him, and can only find one that has been preserved. In this he says:

"DEAREST MOTHER:

"I would have written before, but have not a minute's spare time in the day, and have been engaged every evening.

"I think I am getting to be of more use in the store, for I am kept pretty busy now. I am praying that I may grow in grace unto the perfect man, and I know you are praying for me.

"Uncle James says if Whitall goes to Millville this week, I can go down on Fifth-day, and stay over until Second-day, and then we can go deer-hunting. Ask father to tell Uriah to arrange the hunt. . . . .

"It is getting late, so must close, with lots of love to all the young ones, their names being too numerous to mention.

"I am very lovingly, my dear father and mother, your ever dutiful son, FRANK."

CHAPTER IV.

IN the spring of 1869 we moved up from Millville, intending to make our home in Philadelphia, but going for the summer months to a little cottage which "Grandpa Whitall" had built for his daughters on the lawn of "The Cedars," his country-place near Haddonfield, New Jersey. As Frank's health seemed to suffer somewhat from the close confinement to business, he gave up his position in the counting-room shortly after our removal, and took a few weeks for country rest and rambling.

This little cottage was a happy summer home for our dear boy during the remainder of his short life. His loving grandpa and grandma Whitall delighted to gather around them in the summer all their children and grandchildren, and it made a happy, merry party. Frank was the oldest of twenty grandchildren, and the whole flock were often all together at "The Cedars," and all, from the oldest to the youngest, thought it was about the happiest place in all the world. There were boating, and driving, and riding, and swimming for the older ones; and trees to climb, and brooks to paddle in, for the younger ones, with a donkey to take them on their longer expeditions. The four older grandchildren, Frank and

Whitall, Minnie and Bessie, formed a very congenial and fun-loving quartette, and kept us all alive with their endless expeditions and pleasant adventures. These summer reunions were eagerly anticipated and joyfully remembered from year to year, and made our dear children very happy. And yet through all the light-heartedness and youthful gaiety, our boy did not forget the underlying secret of a heart at peace with God, which so colored and brightened his life. Writing to one of his cousins a year before his death, in reference to the summer reunion, he says:

"And what a responsible position we two hold among our cousins. Just think, we are the only ones who profess to be wholly given up to Christ, and how we shall have to hold up the standard of holiness, and show them that our life is a truly happy one. Do let us pray ever so earnestly for —— and ——. If they could only be made real hearty Christians, what splendid times we 'd have this summer. For after all I don't know of any subject I am so much interested in as Christ."

Thus beautifully did the gospel of joy and peace, which he had heard and believed, bear its legitimate fruit in Frank's heart, making it natural for him to love communion on this subject better than he loved anything else. And the blessed results in his daily life and walk, among the mirthful group of grandchildren at "The Cedars," were such as to win from every one, whether old or young, the same testimony that "Frank never did anything wrong." His cousin W—— used to call him sometimes the "model grandchild," and we would all smile at the name.

But it was indeed true, and Frank's uncles and aunts all feel that, in losing him, their children have lost one who would have been a safe and blessed example to them always. I am glad we did not wait until after his death to know how good he was, and that he himself had the pleasure of hearing from the lips of those who loved him, over and over, what a joy and a comfort he was to all of us. How my heart used to thrill with pride and delight when his grandpa Whitall would say to him sometimes at the close of a happy day at "The Cedars": "Franky dear, when I die, I want thee to remember that thy grandpa never had any fault to find with thee for anything."

Dear grandpa little thought at such times that our strong, healthy, manly boy would be the first to be called home, in the very bloom of his youth, and that the summons would come to him in the midst of one of these happy summers at "The Cedars." It was very sweet to us all, however, that our kind Heavenly Father so arranged it as to let this lovely spot, where Frank had been so happy, be the scene of his last brief illness, and his sudden translation into the far happier and eternally blessed home awaiting him in the better world. If Frank could have chosen himself, I think he would have chosen this. And for the rest of us, we realize that a tie tenderer than ever binds us to the peaceful seclusion of this sweet summer retreat.

During part of the summer of 1869, Frank was at West town boarding-school, having taken a sudden fancy that he would enjoy a few months that summer at a boarding-school. And as usual, we had so much confidence in his principles and his judgment, that we allowed him to follow out his own plans in reference to it. He seemed for a little while to be quite in perplexity as to his decision, but he told us afterward that he asked the Lord to guide his judgment, and that he believed he had decided according to the will of God.

He remained at West town a few months, and then, on account of weak eyes, the result of a serious attack of catarrh some few years before, was obliged to return to "The Cedars" in August of 1869, in order to rest before the winter schools should open.

These few months, however, were much enjoyed by him, and none of us regretted that he had gone. His home letters were very frequent, but not especially interesting to any but his parents, being full of little details of his school life, the croquet and base-ball matches, and the amusements generally in and out of school. A few extracts, however, will show that the blessed Holy Spirit was leading him on step by step into the full light, for which he had begun to long at Millville, and that no surroundings could make him forget his Lord. Writing to his father Fourth-mo. 10th, he says:

"DEAR FATHER:

"Thy acceptable letter came to hand, and I am very much obliged to thee for it. I have indeed been thrown under extraordinary religious influences, and I feel very thankful for it too. But I am a most weak disciple of my *precious* Lord, afraid to do anything to forward His cause for fear of being laughed at. Pray that I may be able to overcome this. It sometimes almost makes me cry, to think of how much Jesus has done for me, and how little I have done in return.

"... I have joined a croquet club, and expect to have a good deal of fun. I enjoy myself here very much, and don't regret that I came at all. Please write to me again, for I feel refreshed and I think strengthened by thy letter of to-day. With heaps of love, I am thy affectionate son, and brother in the Lord, FRANK W. SMITH."

To me he writes, at another time:

"DEAR MOTHER:

"The box came all right, and I am very much obliged for it, also for the Decalcomanias, which are very funny. I am having an elegant time here, and am not at all sorry I came.

"I could resist the temptation no longer, and have joined the first Latin class. We are now reading Virgil; it is elegant fun, almost as nice as reading a story-book. Thee need not be afraid I am studying too much though, for I have plenty of time. . . . . .

"Now as to my Christian experience. I think I am growing in grace some, though not much I am afraid; not as much as I would like. But I am trusting, and I think the good Lord will deliver me from this body of sin, and make me wholly His.

"I wish I could see Alice; the dear little duck-a-daddles! Cover her with kisses. Tell 'rogey-pogey,' I think those drawings she sent me are beautiful; but that I generally try to know my lessons so well that I do not need a fool's-cap. The boys here have sponge-cake sent them (a hint!).

"Dear mother, I will not do anything that will make me go against my conscience, but I see no harm in a little foolish fun, as thee calls it, if I do not think it is wrong.

"With lots of love, and 100,000,000 kisses to 'Bay' and all the children, I am thy loving son,

"FRANKLIN SMITH."

Frank had always been in the habit of taking a little time every morning for reading the Bible and for prayer; but on first going to West town, he wrote to us that he could not keep this up, because he had no private place to go to for the purpose. I suggested the woods at last, and in one of his letters he says. "I find time every morning before breakfast to read my Bible alone in the woods, and it is a great comfort to me. I think the Lord is keeping me, but I am a very weak child of His. I pray for more strength."

He had regretted very much this summer, leaving the merry group of grandchildren at "The Cedars," and especially Minnie, whose home was in Baltimore, and whom he therefore had not many opportunities of seeing. In one of his letters he writes: "The rule of the school is, that those boys who get grade ten for the week, can get out early on Seventh-day. This week there were three, of whom I was one. I went out and sat in the woods, and read poetry, and wrote a piece to Minnie, which I will let thee see.

Thee need not return it, for I have another copy; and thee can put it away, and show it to me some time when I am an old man, and I will laugh at it."

This piece was in imitation of Longfellow's Hiawatha, and was as follows:

"Is my Minnehaha lonely?
Did her Hiawatha leave her?
Well, her Hiawatha 's sorry,
Sorry that he cannot see her,
See his lovely Minnehaha.
And this summer at the Cedars,
Will she think of Hiawatha,
While his light canoe she paddles
On the shining big fresh water?
He has gone to fight the white men
In the land of the Dacotahs;
And all through the days of summer
Will he fight them hardly, hardly;
And when days are growing hazy,
And the leaves from trees are falling,
Will he come back to his wigwam.
In the wild dark woods of Westtown,
I am writing this unto thee.
Gayly near me sings the robin,
And all nature that surrounds me
Is as green and fresh as can be:
But my thoughts are not at Westtown,
Are not with my comrades round me,
For I 'm thinking of Owanee,
And of thee, my Minnehaha.
And I 'm lonely, lonely, lonely,
In the land of the Dacotahs;
There is something that is wanting,
That I may be fully happy,
'Tis *thy* presence, Minnehaha!

HIAWATHA."

After all, however, Frank's weak eyes forced him to return home before the falling of the leaves, and he had a good share of the summer's pleasures with Minnie, and all the grandchildren at the dear old "Cedars."

The ensuing autumn we moved to Philadelphia, and Frank spent the winter at home attending an academy at Broad and Market Streets, preparing himself to enter college the next fall. We have no records left of this winter. It was a busy one for our son, as his year's intermission had thrown him somewhat back in his studies; but he felt that his discipline and training in the counting-room had been very valuable to him, and that he came back to his books with a mind greatly strengthened and matured.

Frank's father was away from home on business a large part of this winter, and his letters to his son were an invaluable part of the influences by which the Lord surrounded this lamb of the flock, who was to be brought so early in his young life into the ripe experience of maturity. The development of his Christian character was not left to the chance influences for good which might, from time to time, surround him. But continually and prayerfully we sought to set before him the only legitimate results of Christian faith, and lovingly and constantly were these pressed upon him. How fully our boy responded to these efforts, and how entirely he satisfied every aspiration we had for him, will be seen as his story goes on.

His father, in writing to him from New Orleans during this winter, says:

"My Precious Son:

"I know not what word to use to express the gushing love I feel for thee as I take my pen; and although the end of three of the hardest days' works I ever did is not just the time to say all that I want to say, I will not wait.

"I thank thee, my darling son, for thy full confidence, which I value. I can only pray for thee, dear boy, and entreat thee to walk in the only easy path; that of *faith-full*-ness. And for this let me give thee a secret of my life, which is this: I find that the first moment the Holy Spirit points out anything to be done, *that* moment is the easy one to do it in. The next moment will find it harder. A third may lead to disobedience. Act easily, because at once.

"Dear Frank, thee is young, in full health, and in prosperous circumstances,—few are so blessed. Thy Heavenly Father so loves His own glory in thy life, and thy own highest happiness, that He cannot suffer thee to take thy rest in the world. I believe that He now calls to thee 'Give me thy heart!' Thy *whole* heart, with all its hopes and joys. It would be so lovely to see thee, with all bright around thee, yield all in a full consecration to Him who bought thee. But if thy heart refuses, what would be the highest token of a Father's love and care? Would it not be to break into pieces thy idols, whatever thee may be setting before thyself apart from Christ, and to bring thee, even though weeping and broken-hearted, to the foot of the cross? How much lovelier to give Him an as yet unbroken spirit, than to wait for the discipline of sorrow to be sent!

"Weigh these things, and the Lord give thee understanding. My heart clings to thee as thee can never know. But, dearly as I love thee, my son, I love God's glory in thee above all; and I love thy highest happiness so much, that sooner would I see thee broken-hearted before the cross, with thy earthly hopes in the dust, but thy heart happy in Jesus, than to see thee in the highest outward prosperity, thy heart's evil desires granted, but leanness in thy soul!

"Thy loving, praying, *sympathizing* father,

"ROBERT PEARSALL SMITH."

The longings of his father's heart here expressed were all in time wonderfully fulfilled, and our son did a little later give the Lord his unbroken spirit; and in the midst of all the brightness of youth and health he yielded himself up in full consecration to Him who had bought him for His own.

But the time was not quite yet. He was to realize yet more fully the vanity of all earthly things, and was to be made to hunger and thirst more deeply for the blessed rest of the life hid with Christ in God.

In September, 1870, he entered Haverford College as a Freshman, full of joyous anticipations of a college life; a happy, good boy, earnestly longing to enter into the fulness of rest and victory, of which he had first heard at Millville, in the year 1867, and for which ever since he had been praying and striving, but not yet having realized it. A few weeks before going, he wrote to one who had also been long seeking the same blessing: "Thee really has that experience thee has sought after for so long, has thee? Do pray that I may have it too. I am longing for it, thee don't know how much."

And this longing seemed but to deepen and strengthen as time went on. The various occupations of his student life interested him much, and he entered with all his heart into the College pleasures, greatly enjoying being "rushed" by the Sophomores, and entering with hearty zest into the "pillow fights" and the cricket and base-ball matches; but through it all there seemed ever to be a continually increasing hunger and thirst after righteousness, and a growing realization that he could never rest satisfied short of the fulness of the salvation that was to be found in Jesus.

Dear Frank knew himself to be a child of God, and felt great peace in believing that all the *guilt* of his sins had been atoned for by the death of the Lord Jesus, and their every stain washed away in His precious blood. But he was conscious that the *power* of sin had not yet been altogether broken in his soul, and that his life was too much passed in an experience that could best be described by Romans vii. 19, 21: "When I would do good, evil is present with me," "for the good that I would I do not, and the evil that I hate that do I." He knew there was a better experience in store for the Christian than this. He had seen it in his tutor during the memorable year of 1867 at Millville. He had known of it in many of his father's workmen. He had heard of it continually from those he loved and honored. Above all, he had been taught to find it in the Bible. He had been long seeking to realize it for himself; and now the blessed Holy Spirit was stirring him up to a longing that would take no denial, and was not to cease until, in the early part of the year 1871, our darling boy learned the secret of a life of faith, and entered upon the blessed highway of holiness, never again to leave it for any lower pathway, until it landed him safe in heaven itself.

In a letter to me, written in November of 1870, which will best show the working of his mind on this subject, he says:

"Once for all I will tell thee freely how I stand at present religiously,—strictly secret, remember. There is nothing I could wish for more than to be sanctified wholly, but I *cannot* give up my will. If I should give it up, and I have often tried to, I feel that I should have to give up so much that I can't do it. For instance, —— says that a sanctified Christian can never be jolly again, nor play any more games. Now I have a perfect horror of this. I have an ambition to become the best at out-door games and all that. And it seems as if I *could* not consent to keep all the rules of this institution. Our class, for instance, expect to "rush" the freshmen next year a good deal. (Thee need not tell any one this, and I am only telling thee on condition that thee won't stop me from doing it.) Now it seems to me that if I made any great profession of sanctification here in the College, the fellows would think it rather inconsistent if I should go right off and break the strictest rule in the whole catalogue. I attend the Bible class because thee and father want me to, and because I think I ought to. Last First-day evening the fellows were building bonfires around the house, which of course is positively forbidden. I did not join in because it was First-day, and I am not quite so bad as to break the Sabbath. But if it had not been First-day, nothing could have prevented me. Had it been Seventh-day night, I should have done it; and then the next evening I would have gone up to the Bible class, like the most consistent fellow here. If I should make any particular profession, it would not seem very consistent, would it? That is where I stand, and where I am afraid I am likely to stand, unless I get stirred up most wonderfully. I am often very much frightened at my position, but it seems I *cannot* change. My prayers at night are cold, heartless forms, more for this world's good things than for spiritual blessings. I suppose all thee can do is to pray for me, for I know the doctrine of sanctification, and all about it, by heart, so often have I heard it. I know you all say it makes you so much happier, but you did not have it while you were as young as I am."

In this letter, our dear boy stated exactly the difficulties of a young heart, when the subject of entire dedication is urged upon it, and we realized that to him they were actual difficulties, needing very careful and tender dealing. I replied to him therefore very fully, trying to show him that the path of dedication was meant to be one of joy, and not one of hardness and suffering; and that if he would only begin at the right end of it, all would come out happily.

My reply was as follows:

"Eleventh-mo. 14th.

"My Darling Boy:

"I am very glad thee writes to me so freely. But I am sorry consecration looks so hard to thee. I know it is natural, and I can sympathize with thy feelings, for I used to feel so myself. But I see plainly where thy mistake is. It is just because thee does not know the *joys* of God's salvation, and therefore the *duties* connected with it appall thee. I wish, my precious boy, that thee would just pray now for one thing, — that God will give thee the *joys* of His salvation. I will ask this for thee, and thee must ask it for thyself. It is not a long prayer, and thee can easily remember to say it morning and evening, and when once thy soul is filled with joy, all the rest will come right. Thee is looking at the thing now in a very legal way, and making the gospel out to be bondage. Whereas, really and truly it is the greatest liberty; and one of its chief elements is joy. Dear Frank, the gospel is good news, a blessed story to make people happy, not a sentence to condemn them to hard and sad servitude. Thee never can know all about it until thee gets hold of it at the right end, the end beginning with 'Love, joy, and peace.' Remember these are the *first* mentioned in that long list of the fruits of the Spirit. Ask for these before thee begins to look forward to the other things. Don't be afraid of the dear Lord; He wants to make thee happy, and will not cut thee off from anything but what would harm thee."

In reference to the mistaken ideas of ——, I told Frank that the Bible never taught that we were to be taken out of the world by becoming Christians, but only that we were to be kept from the evil in it, that religion was not meant to make us unnatural, nor to turn a boy into an old man. And I assured him that all innocent games and amusements would be just as lawful to him after being consecrated, as before, the only difference being that he could enjoy them with a free conscience and a happy heart.

But as to breaking the rules, I told him it was always unmanly and very foolish, and could win respect from no one; that a law-abiding citizen was always the honored and trusted one, and that the boy who aimed at future positions of confidence must begin, therefore, by being a law-abiding student. And finally I urged him to compare the joys of a consecrated life with the uneasiness and self-reproaches that must necessarily follow a course of disobedience to lawful authority.

It will be seen from our boy's letter that he was always very honest with himself. And in truth he was so careful never to say more than was strictly true, that we often thought his danger lay in the other direction, and that a more free and unconstrained expression of his religious experience would have been more helpful to himself and to others. This careful honesty, however, now renders doubly valuable every after word of his concerning the wonderful victory he so soon realized over the very difficulties mentioned in this early letter. His confessions of what the Lord did for his soul were always behind rather than beyond the reality.

CHAPTER V.

HE stirring up which he expressed the need of, came to him not long afterwards, and came, in the wonderful grace of God, through joy and not through sorrow. Frank's uncle and aunt, Horace J. and Margaret L. Smith, lived at Hestonville, about five miles from Haverford College, and with generous kindness they gave Frank the treat of a party at their house every three weeks on Saturday afternoons. Frank was to invite some of his fellow-students to accompany him, and I was to take out with me from the city a few of his young cousins and friends to join them.

Our first party was on October 8th, 1870, and was the beginning of a succession of the pleasantest, happiest reunions of young people it was ever my lot to attend. "Uncle Horry" and "Aunt Maggie" made us feel thoroughly welcome and at home, and the merry out-door games in the afternoon, and the evening's innocent amusements in-doors, will never be forgotten by any who shared in them. The little party, who met thus from time to time, called themselves in merriment "Heston-villains," and were drawn together in a close bond of youthful friendship that was to us elders delightful to witness and join in.

It was through these parties, and what grew out of them, that Frank's awakening was to come. Nearly all of the young circle were Christians, and one or two of them were truly consecrated in heart and life to the service of their Lord. And the joyous merriment of their games and their talk seemed never to turn their hearts away from a far deeper interest in the blessed subject of the glorious salvation they had found in the Lord Jesus Christ. The gospel had come to them all, as a piece of good news to make them happy, and not as a code of severe laws to frighten them and make them sad. And the ending to their happy evenings which they all loved the best, was to gather in Uncle Horry's parlors, around the glowing fire, and read the Bible and sing hymns together, followed by a little season of silent waiting before the Lord, in which some of the young voices would be heard breaking the silence in prayer or simple confession. It was the influence of these little meetings which at last effectually awakened our boy.

The first of these occasions however was held in our own parlor in Filbert Street, where we gathered one evening on our return from Hestonville, while waiting for the late train that was to carry our students back to their college. Frank's father proposed our each one telling the present state of our religious experience, and began asking one after another some simple question to draw it out. He turned to Frank first, and our dear boy was thus obliged to come out openly, and declare upon whose side he was, which he ever after felt to have been a great blessing to him. It was a deeply solemn and touching occasion. As one after another uttered their simple confession of blessing or of need, scarcely a dry eye remained in the room, and two of the Haverford students broke down entirely, saying they were not converted, but that there was nothing which they longed for so much.

In reference to this evening one of the young ladies has written to us since Frank's death:

"My religious friendship with Frank began that evening, after one of our first Hestonville parties, when we walked in to Philadelphia, and met in your parlor for confession and prayer. I think he was the first young man with whom I had ever had a religious conversation, and it was a great strength to both of us. We spoke of the great need of Haverford, and the great work to be done there, and, when we parted on our steps, agreed that we would each pray for the College, until the Lord should bless it. And his faith was very strengthening to my own; he said he saw no reason why we should not receive an answer to our prayer."

The result of this little season was, that the two dear boys spoken of were converted within a few days, and that they were all so much interested as to beg Frank's father to come out to Haverford sometimes to talk to them and help them on their Christian pathway. He gladly consented, and from that time occasionally met a few of Frank's cousins and fellow-students in a room belonging to one of the Professors at the College. In these little social meetings, the attention of those present was first called to the certainty of the forgiveness of sin to those who put their full trust in the atoning work of the Lord Jesus. And a number of intelligent and earnest young men there for the first time found peace in believing. At the same time there was pressed upon those who, like Frank, had realized this joy of forgiveness, that it was their privilege to know in their own experience an entire inward consecration of will, and a full trust in Christ's power to keep them from sin. They were led to place themselves in the searching light of the Holy Spirit, asking that every thought and desire, the very central powers of their existence, might be brought into conformity to the will of God. Many an unsanctified ambition and unholy feeling, scarcely defined in the comparative twilight of their previous experience, was here brought into the light of consciousness, and yielded to God. And several of them, during the course of these meetings, and while under the sweet influences of the Hestonville parties, in large measure entered upon this higher experience of Christian privilege, and realized in their souls a uniformity of love, joy and peace, with a corresponding outward consistency of life, such as they had not before known. Our own precious boy was among this number, as will be seen from his letters; and from that time his Christian character shone brighter and brighter, until the coming to him of the perfect day.

Perhaps one of the most important features of these meetings to the young Christians, was the vocal confession they there made of Christ as their Saviour. Some who had long been trusting Him, but who had never defined to themselves, nor confessed to others the blessed fact that they were therefore the children of

God, found in these simple confessions the undying assurance of a Saviour's love; and realized the blessedness promised, in Rom. x. 10, to those who not only believe in their hearts, but also confess with their mouths, the Lord Jesus. Our dear Frank here learned the importance of this Christian duty of confession, and was enabled afterwards, when among strangers at Princeton College, to bear a faithful testimony to his Lord and Saviour Jesus Christ.

A few extracts from his letters and diary of this winter will reveal the sweet development of his Christian experience, and will show how, through it all, he was the real boy, turning easily after a boy's fashion from grave to gay, mingling his College games and his religious feelings in the most natural sort of way, and finding out the blessed truth that the more he learned of the salvation of Jesus, the more perfectly he found it was suited to him as a boy, with a boy's needs and a boy's difficulties. Never to the very last did he cease to be a boy. And it was one of the crowning charms of his Christian experience that it never made him unnatural, nor deprived him of the hearty healthy enjoyment of his young life, with all its innocent pleasures and pursuits.

We tried to impress upon his mind that he was to enter into the sports belonging to his time of life heartily and with an unclouded conscience; that in the divinely arranged harmony of things, he at his age was as much called to the development of his character, physical, moral, and intellectual, by throwing himself with heartiness into all innocent sports congenial to his years and tastes, as his parents were called to bend themselves to the work of life. We taught him to enter upon the cricket-field, or the foot-ball match, as thoroughly in communion with his Lord as in his moments of sober work. And he learned the lesson. So that afterwards in writing to one of his friends, he said, that when his eyes were looking to the Lord, and his trust in Him was unwavering, he could enter with his whole heart into all the pleasures around him, but that when his communion was clouded, he could not enjoy even the most exciting cricket-match that ever was played.

On the 30th of October, 1870, Frank wrote in reference to the Hestonville party of the day before :

"DARLING MOTHER :

"I think yesterday was a perfect success ; as far as we Haverford students are concerned, I know it was. The fellows all said that they had a capital time. We have already begun to look forward to the next time. I hope Bay is not sick. It made me feel real bad not to be able to pay more attention to her and Alice and Logan ; in fact, I felt quite homesick when I got back here. I am ever so glad I had that little talk with thee. Although we did not say much, yet it seemed so much like home to talk to thee confidentially as in olden times. With us College fellows it always is a long, long while ago since we were school-boys, thee knows. Does thee think the girls liked it? Try and find out. I hope I impressed them with a faint idea of how humble my position as a Freshman is, and how exalted that of my companions as Juniors pretends to be."

About the same date he wrote to his "Aunty Lill":

"My Dearest Aunty:

"I was very glad indeed to see thee at Hestonville, for I hardly expected thee would come. I wish I could have seen more of thee, but the young ladies had to be attended to.

"I was also very glad to hear of N.'s conversion, but as to writing to her, as thee asks me to, that is altogether out of the question. I would as soon think of flying. In the first place, I know that I am too cold a Christian, and do not feel as if it would be genuine feeling, even if I should write. I am very sorry to make this confession, but I am afraid it is too true. I don't know what message I could send to her, either. I am of course very glad to hear of her conversion. I have been praying for her ever since I was certain she was not a Christian. I hope she will be more faithful than I have been."

As yet our boy was only experiencing the convictions of the Holy Spirit, revealing to him his cold condition. And meanwhile many other interests were filling up his young life.

He had not forgotten the "S. S. S." Society in his new associations, and about this time he wrote the following epistle to the absent members, on the occasion of the meaning of their name having been discovered:

"Dear Companions of my Youth:

"To be writing you an epistle in this manner reminds me of my youthful days, so long ago, before I entered here as a College student. I often think of those days with pleasure, and with many regrets that they are gone to me. For of course a College student is not expected to play any more, nor to do anything unpractical. If he hunts for arbutus, it is for the good of his botany. If he rows, it is for the sake of his muscle. If he plays hare and hound, he does it to improve his lungs. But as for doing such frivolous things as walk fences, ride in a donkey-cart, build dams, or anything of that sort, they are all out of the question. He may perhaps skate once in a while, to relieve his overburdened mind; but he scarcely ever does it with ladies, as it would make him unfit to study.

"My dignity as such a person has suffered considerably since coming here by being 'rushed.' The Sophomores seem scarcely to remember that I am as good as they, and maybe, better; and the way they have 'hazed' me, considering who I am, is too frightful to relate. Prof. —— also made me feel rather badly by catching me in the middle of a pillow-fight the other evening, into which you may be sure I did not enter of my own accord, but was forced into it by my antagonist hitting me first.

"I have to study four hours a day, and am leading well the tail of the class, a high position, the class consisting of eight, and there being but seven above me.

"I also am so great a favorite here that all the students rival each other in seeing who can be with me most, and I, fearing to be partial, am constrained to go alone a great deal.

"Now I hope I have impressed you with a due sense of my great dignity. For let me tell you, it always leaves an impression wherever it goes. If you were to see me, I have no doubt you would be surprised at its magnitude.

"And now let us attend to some society business. Our name, that name which has always inspired us with a desire for mischief, that name which above all others was so suited to our characters, has been found out! What shall we do? The matter is serious. It requires careful consideration by the thinking part of our members; and much of the thinking part, you will of course allow, is vested in the College student, or, in other words, in the dignified writer. His opinion therefore is, that we should have a new name, and take more precautions to keep it secret. Think it over, ye frivolous sub-freshmen, and let me hear your decision.

"Hoping you will feel honored by this remarkable condescension on my part, in writing to you small children, I remain, your truly dutiful servant,

"F. W. SMITH."

On December 4th, he writes:

"DARLING MOTHER:

"It hardly seems worth while to write to thee after having written so lately, but still I'll do it. In the first place let me tell thee about my good grade for last month. I was perfectly astounded. Happily for my nerves, I don't believe it will happen again. This was it: Six hundred and ninety-eight and three quarters — seven hundred being perfect; that is, I said every lesson through the month perfect except two. Is n't it astounding? The fellow who was second in the class had six hundred and ninety-two for his grade, six and three-quarters lower than mine. Please don't faint on reading this, for I 'll never do it again, so excuse me!

"We had — at least I had — an extremely pleasant evening when father was out. For the first time in my life I prayed out-loud, and I felt glad afterwards I had done it; that is, I think I felt a certain degree of peace. But I am sorry to say, it is all gone now, and I am the same as ever, cold and — thee knows it all."

During the visit here referred to, Frank's father suggested to the young men that it would be a great help and strength to them to have a little prayer-meeting together, at such times as he could not be with them; and in Frank's next letter of December 7th, he thus speaks of these meetings:

"About our little meeting — we have it from 12 to 12.20 every day. It is a curious fact that they are the nicest meetings I was ever at; in fact, I quite look forward to them, more than I can say of any other meeting I ever attended. What is the reason? Because I take part? I think we would rather conduct the meeting as we do now than any other way. One of us reads a few verses from the Bible; and then we wait on the Lord for guidance, and some one prays and some one else speaks. It is very interesting."

On December 25th, he wrote:

"DEAREST MOTHER:

"How I did long to be at home last night, to see the children and you, and the Christmas-tree, and all. If I had not made up my mind not to be, I should have been real homesick. Did you have a nice time? And are there any more presents for me?

"As father has probably told thee, we are about to start a Bible class among ourselves. We expect persecution when all we do is found out, but I think the Lord will help us to stand it for His sake. I am afraid I don't live very consistently, but I hardly feel ready to give up all my fun, and strictly obey all the rules; it looks like a life of such awful bondage."

The year 1870 closed on our boy, leaving him still in what was to himself a very unsatisfactory state of experience, though outwardly to us he was, as always, the same dear, good, noble fellow, who had rejoiced our home and our hearts for so many years. The year 1871 opened upon him in very much the same state of mind.

On January 8th, 1871, he wrote:

"I think the fellows all enjoyed father's talk the other night. R. says he could listen any length of time; he is really deeply interested in the subject of sanctification. He says I am the only person he ever talked to on religious subjects, except his sister. There are almost too many in the room, when father comes out, for them to talk freely to him; however, I don't see how it can be remedied. Our meetings now are pretty lively. T. made a beautiful prayer, the other day; and quite often, he and H. make some remark on some passage in the Bible.

"I can't tell thee exactly what I mean by being inconsistent. Nothing very glaring, I suppose, but a general feeling that I am inconsistent, with such a high profession as I make here, by going to and taking part in these meetings. And I fear I never can feel that I am in the least consistent, until I give up and become sanctified. But the giving up, it seems, I *cannot* do. There are perhaps only two things that I cling to very strongly, but it seems as if I could not give them up. Nearly everything else I can give up pretty easily, but these two I cannot. They are comparatively very small things in themselves, and thee would most likely consider them nothing, but they are just where my will sticks."

Again, on the 15th of January, he wrote:

"All the boys enjoyed father's visit last week, but it don't seem to have had any effect on the meetings. R. and I are the only ones who are apparently stirred up about them. We have determined to do our duty in them, and although it don't do much good, still it can't help having some effect, however little. R. is really deeply interested. We had a long talk yesterday, and at last we came to the conclusion that we would be more happy, and more useful in every way, if we would only consecrate ourselves wholly. And he said he would, if I would. But it really seemed as if I *could not* give up my will. Perhaps I shall be able to, some time. I cannot help thinking what blessed results would most likely come in the college if there were even two of the Lord's weakest ones given up to Him. And as R. said,—'Would I not be willing to give up everything to save one soul?' It does seem as if I could at the time, and yet when the thing comes up, immediately I retract."

The next day he wrote:—"Thee must not tell any one, please, because I hate any great profession, and then a coming short of it; but last night I believe the Lord enabled me to give up all my hold on the world, and abandon myself wholly to Him."

From this time the work went rapidly on in our dear boy's heart. The first giving up of his will did not, it is true, reach down into the inmost depths of his life, and he found afterwards many and far greater things to be abandoned to the Lord. But it was the *beginning* of a life consecrated to God, and thenceforth his path was steadily onward and upward.

On the 17th I replied to this:

"My Darling Boy:

"I seize the first moment I have had to answer thy precious letter, and cannot express to thee how it rejoiced my heart. Oh, dear Frank, there may not be any rapturous joy in thus abandoning thyself to thy Saviour for Him to do with thee according to His own will, but there is always peace, and that is enough. Thee must watch now against discouragement. Remember my favorite quotation from George Fox, that 'all discouragement is from the Evil One;' and no matter what thy difficulties or perplexities may be, let them never for a moment cause thee to be discouraged. Afresh abandon thyself to the Lord, and afresh believe that He does receive thee, and undertake thy case. It is just too lovely to think of thee as belonging altogether to Him now, and to know how happy He will make thee! And thee must be just as simple and light-hearted as a little child; have no cares and no fears; but let Jesus carry every burden, and take every trouble. Faber says:

'If our faith were but more simple,
We would take Him at His word,
And our lives would be all sunshine
In the presence of our Lord.'"

Our boy's next letter shows us by what a sad experience he learned the necessary lesson, that, while with the heart man believeth unto righteousness, with the mouth confession must be made unto salvation. It will tell its own story.

"Dearest Mother:

"Thee knows I told thee last Second-day that I had given up all. Well, all that morning I felt peaceful and happy, until I went up to our little meeting, and there it came to me that I should confess that I had consecrated myself. But then I thought, 'Suppose I fall, how will it look after having made such a high profession?' Which immediately shut me up. Consequently I began to lose my peace, and the next day it was all gone. It was the same for two or three days, until by Sixth-day evening I was so weak, that I entirely gave way to my temper, more than I have done before for a year or so; and on account of this giving way, have made myself miserable, and estranged two of my best friends in the college. It is my place to go and make up, as I did the getting mad; but it is such fearfully hard work, that I don't know whether I can possibly do it. If I don't do it, it won't be done, and it will make the whole class uncomfortable, as this is the first quarrel any of us have had. I feel dreadfully about it. Why is it that as soon as I try to give up and walk in a really Christian way, I immediately fall? It is mighty humbling, anyhow. Perhaps I did not trust enough. But I have not any faith, hardly enough even to pray for more. I'm all in a muddle, and don't know how to get out."

In the little pocket-diary Frank kept this year,—the only one he ever kept that we can find,—in which he noted down briefly whatever interested him, he wrote, January 20th:

"Very poor skating. Half holiday. Began bracket. Got mad at —— and ——."

On the 26th he wrote:

"Thermometer 5°. Heavy snow all day. Made up with —— and ——. Spent afternoon in one of the Professors' room, with them and ——. Jolly fun. Sang, and had a nice time generally."

Between these two entries he had written me the letter quoted above, and we had met at one of the Hestonville parties, where I had had a little conversation with him about it. I found he was very much discouraged, and in fact I had hardly ever seen our dear boy so sad as he seemed that night. He felt as if it was all of no use: he never could live a holy life, and he might as well give it up in despair. I showed him where the beginning of his trouble lay, in having failed to acknowledge his consecration in the meeting, when the Spirit had prompted him. I reminded him of the passage which says, "With the heart man believeth unto righteousness, and with the mouth confession is made unto salvation," and of the promise to those who confess with the mouth and believe in the heart, that they "shall be saved." And told him, I thought this meant, that salvation could not be fully realized until confession was made; that many had lost their consecration from a failure to acknowledge it, and that he would never have any strength until he was willing to do the Lord's will in this respect.

But I told him that there was no cause for discouragement whatever; that we find in the Bible a provision for just such a case, "If any man sin, we have an advocate with the Father, even Jesus Christ the righteous;" and, "If we confess our sins, He is faithful and just to forgive us our sins, and to cleanse us from all unrighteousness." I told Frank that it very often happened, when Satan found souls seeking to escape from his bondage, that he tripped them up in a most unexpected way, in order to discourage them, and make them give up the struggle. But that he might completely baffle Satan by going at once to the Lord for the promised forgiveness and cleansing; and then, being reconciled to God, he could go and be reconciled with his brother. The dear boy's brow cleared as we talked, and he did at once, then and there, confess his sin to his Heavenly Father, and believe he was forgiven, according to the word. But there still remained the duty of reconciliation with his brother, and of this he wrote to me on January 29th.

"DEAREST MOTHER:

"In the first place, about my experience. I had the most *awful* time making up my mind to say anything to those two boys, that I ever had in my life. I thought about it, and prayed about it, and scolded myself that it was not either gentlemanly, or Christian like, until at last, when on Fourth-day I had spoken to only one of them, I felt so perfectly unhappy that I believe I could have done something desperate. But that night I prayed for strength to do it the next day, and I prayed for about half an hour, until at last faith was given me, and the next morning I did it; so now we are better friends than ever. But still I am not at all at rest; and yet I believe I have given up everything, except one thing, and I don't know whether I am required to give that up or not. The thought just struck me the other day, 'Am I willing to speak in the meeting at the meeting-house, if I felt called on to do it?' I do not think I can ever give that up, if I am required. That *may* be my sticker, I don't know. But if it is, I don't know how I am going to get over it. I am perfectly willing to say anything in our little meetings up-stairs, but I cannot speak publicly before the whole college, in a regular meeting. It is impossible. However, I 'll see thee soon and talk about all such things. And now for gossip."

In his diary, under date of February 12th, while paying a visit during vacation at Baltimore, he writes:

"Went with M. and B. and heard Caroline Talbot preach a first-rate sermon. Good talk on my future prospects with M. I should like to be a lawyer, that I might have some chance of being a mover in a great reformation of our country."

Frank's cousin M. was the recipient of all his aspirations and hopes in life. No plan was ever matured by him, until it was first talked over with her. She supplied to him almost more than a sister's place, sympathizing in all his tastes, and rousing him into a love for all that was noble and pure in literature and in morals, and making his life bright with her energetic spirits and her hearty appreciation of fun. Almost the last thing they were doing together at "The Cedars," the week before he was taken sick, was reading aloud to one another Milton's *Paradise Lost*, and planning together to have a sailboat on the creek near the place. Such perfect sympathy as existed between them must, I think, be rare between cousins, and it was one of the chief joys of our boy's life.

CHAPTER VI.

ON the 26th of February Frank wrote:

"DARLING MOTHER:

"I verily believe, if father had not come out last week, our meetings would have been dropped, for a little while at least. His coming stirred us up some, and that night R. and I prayed that we might have an especially good meeting on Seventh-day, and we had faith too. But, by the way, tell father he made a remark that C. needed very much: the one on never arguing with an unbeliever about Bible doctrines. C. does that continually, arguing about predestination for instance, with ——, and I believe it must be a drawback to his saving any souls.

"But to continue. Seventh-day we went up, and there were eight of us. In the beginning, R. proposed that we should all kneel down when any one prayed. H. modified by saying, Such as did not approve of it, of course need not do it. Well, we sat in silence a very little while, and then H. kneeled down to pray, and every one else kneeled but two. When H. was through, and he prayed feelingly as he always does, we remained on our knees; just think of that for us! In a little while I prayed, then four others.

Then we rose, and after a little while, S. said that he was happy to be able to confess that, on Sixth-day night, after being in the meeting with father, he had for the first time gone down with a feeling that he did not want to sneak into the collecting-room. H. said the same, and then we closed the first really lively meeting we ever held up there.

"Ask the girls if they won't pray, especially that we may have a greater degree of brotherly love toward each other, for we cannot work without it. I was speaking to one of them about it last Third-day."

The next day he wrote:

"I guess I'll have to give up all hopes of consecration for the present, for I cannot give up my will in the matter of publicly confessing in the meeting-house. To-day, —— got up, and said there, before every one, that he was able to say he was on the Lord's side. Every one was deeply impressed."

On March 5th he wrote:

"Our meetings continue very good. Very free and easy, and to me sometimes very powerful. I am just beginning to see that a Christian's life can be a happy one, a thing I never realized before. It always seemed to me that a Christian must be talking awfully good, and acting awful sober all the time, and after all be somewhat of a hypocrite. But I see now it is not at all necessary.

"How does thee know, dear mother, that we ought to pray in every meeting? I am afraid I take too much on myself, for I do more now in our little meetings than some others. We were getting dead again the other day,—had had two silent meetings, and I felt thoroughly stirred up, so I kneeled down and prayed that we might be 'roused from our deadness.' Did I do right? Yesterday we had a very good meeting, for the first time praying for ourselves individually, that we each one might have our last stumbling-block removed. Do tell me about prayer in thy next letter."

In reply I wrote:

"Prayer is not a sort of religious performance, to be entered upon only when we feel in a good state of mind. It is simply asking for something we want. And the time to pray is when you realize your need of anything, and this often happens when you do not feel any particular comfort in praying. There is never a hint anywhere in the Bible that we are to wait for any especial feeling in order to pray, except the feeling of need. Everywhere we are told to *ask*, not to *feel*. A great many people think their prayers will not be heard, unless they feel very fervent and tender. But God does not hear our prayers because of our feelings at all, but because of the plea we bring, even the precious availing plea of Jesus' blood, and we can bring this plea even in our coldest and deadest moments. Whatever you want, *ask for it*, for the promise is, 'Ask and ye *shall* receive.' When I go into a meeting, I always ask God to give me a sense of the needs of the meeting, and when I feel these, then I believe it is right for me to pray, unless some one else does."

In Frank's next letter he says:

"Please send me some texts, proving what thee wrote about praying, that I may bring them up at our next little Bible class, as the lesson is on Prayer. Suppose, too, thee sends me some lessons for the First-day evening Bible class, and maybe there will be a chance of having them some time.

"It has got out somehow that we pray for the fellows by name up-stairs in our meetings, and one fellow came up to —— the other day, as mad as could be, and said, 'Do you ever pray for me up-stairs?' —— told him if he wanted to know to come up and see. 'Well,' he said, 'if you pray for me, I'll skin you alive.' Rather strong language, was n't it?"

Under date of March 9th is the following entry in his pocket diary:

"Letter from Bay. I do love those little things like everything. Find it out when I get away from home. I must answer the letter very soon, for I know how she likes to get letters. Read a little out of Ruskin. Found in him what I have always wanted, — a list of books that ought to be read. Every spare minute I intend to read up on literature. I want very much to read the standard works."

On March 15th he wrote to his father:

"My Darling Father:

"I am up very early this morning on purpose to write to thee. So please prize my letter.

"It seems quite a dreary prospect to look forward to not seeing thee out here this week. I am so used to it now, and I do enjoy thy visits so much. Thy coming has done *me* spiritually an infinite amount of good. Before thee began to come, I used to think that I never could learn anything more of thee, as I had heard thee talk so often. But I have found my mistake. Instead of looking on the Christian life as a stiff, constrained, and solemn one, I see that it can be very natural and joyous. Well, I saw a sign the other day that I am called a good many names behind my back, for what I do. It was this. I left a book lying in one of the class-rooms, and the next time I saw it, it had written all over the cover, 'Franky Smith, the Prayer-meeting Genius.' It was a considerable trial to me to bear it patiently, but the Lord helped me.

"And now about our meetings. I hardly know what to say. I wish somebody would take an eleven-pronged pole and poke us all up. At my request, mother sent out a great number of texts, urging constant prayer on us. I read them in our meeting, and said that I hoped no one of us would feel that he had to wait for a great moving before prayer, but would follow a gentle impression. But it did not seem to have any effect. I say so much in our meetings, trying to get them roused up, that I am afraid they won't like it.

"One of the fellows here takes a very sad view of the Christian life, which, as I understand it, is one of joy. In talking to some one the other day, he told him he thought a Christian ought never to joke, nor laugh, nor be anything but sober all the time. That he ought not to have anything to do with unbelievers, except to preach to them. This latter point he brought up in our meeting, and enforced it on us as being absolutely necessary for a Christian. We all went against him, and said we thought that if we let unbelievers alone, except just to preach to them, they would not hear our message. He quoted the text, 'Come out from among them and be ye separate, saith the Lord;' and we interpreted it to mean, Be separate in spirit, that is, do not countenance their evil deeds. Were we right? His seems a very hard view of the Christian life.

"I am getting along nicely in my studies. The smartest fellow in the senior class said to me yesterday, that nothing would give him greater pleasure than if I would read my Virgil with him. He said he had heard I was a smart classical scholar, and that he thought he could learn as much from me as I could from him. I am afraid he will be disappointed.

"In haste, with love, I am thy 'owney doney' son,

"FRANK."

On March 29th, Frank wrote:

"DARLING MOTHER:

"Thee has got me into the scrape, and now thee must get me out of it. I have been appointed to lead in the First-day evening Bible class; and now thee must send out a lesson for me. Make a really stirring and interesting one, that will attract the boys to listen to it. Now be sure, and send it soon, so that I can study it first."

On April 2d we received a letter from our boy that filled our hearts with unspeakable joy. It was written the next day after one of the monthly Hestonville parties, when the boys had chosen to miss the train and walk home the five miles, for the sake of an hour more at "Uncle Horry's." It had been a sweet evening, full of innocent merriment, and ending in a precious little meeting, never to be forgotten.

"My Darling Mother:

"There is so much to say to-day, that I hardly know where to begin. But here goes. In the first place, after wading through an unmentionable quantity of mud and mire, on our way home from Hestonville last night, we at last arrived here safely. Oh! but we did feel tired, and wet, and muddy. But we all exclaimed with one voice, that the last hour more than paid for the walk. We did just have a splendid time. And, thanks to a really sensible talk I had with Miss ——, I never enjoyed an evening so much in my life. How immeasurably better it was than to talk to some frivolous nonsensical girl of the world.

"Now I suppose thee would like to have me hold an experience meeting with thee, wouldn't thee? Here it is. In the first place, some time last week I think it was, I felt my need of entire consecration deeply, and my principal point of difficulty seemed to be that I was afraid of man, and was not willing to be made anything for Christ's sake. Well, I told it to ——, and he advised me to tell it in the meeting, saying he would pray for me. The next day I did, asking for their prayers. But I did not seem to change much until Fifth-day, when Samuel Emlen was out here. Mother, never in all my life have I heard a sermon as eloquent, as really inspired as that sermon was. To hear him, standing up there, with his splendid voice showing forth the joys of a Christian life, compared to one of the world; and the joys of an entirely consecrated Christian life, compared to that of a half-hearted Christian; and say with all his earnestness, 'Seek ye first the kingdom of God, and *all* things necessary *shall* be added,' was altogether too much for me. I gave right in, gave up my fear of man, and all, to Christ. Well, I got through that day happily; but in the evening I joined in some mischief that was against the rules, and one thing and another, so I was put back somewhat. Then I was not faithful in speaking to some unconverted fellows. So I came to Hestonville yesterday, ready for a great deal of good. I got Miss —— over in the corner, and there she told me her experience, and I told her mine, and we tried to comfort each other. She told me I *must* have more faith, and that she was going to pray for me that I might get it. And so last night, after reaching home, I concluded there was no use holding out any longer; I must be either a whole-hearted Christian or none. And I had my choice; I must choose one. I was helped to choose the whole-hearted Christian course, and give myself altogether to the Lord. I just said, 'Lord, take from me everything, only give me Thyself.' H. has consecrated himself too; so this afternoon, from two until four, H., S., and I are all going to meet together to pray for a blessing to-morrow. I am absolutely certain we will get it, so I will not send this letter until after that time, or rather until after we get our blessing."

"SECOND-DAY, 8 O'CLOCK.

"We had our meeting yesterday, and I tell thee I never was so blessed in all my life; nor did I ever enjoy anything so much as I did that little meeting. We went into one of the class-rooms, and before we knelt down, we told each other that we were willing to give up everything to the Lord. Then we knelt, and told God we gave Him our all, and specified some of the things; and we pleaded His promise that we should have all our wants satisfied if we believed. And we did believe, so that before we went out of the room, we not only knew that we ourselves were blessed, but we also believed that our meeting to-day would be wonderfully blessed; and that one, for whom we prayed, would be converted soon. So we had a glorious time.

"5 O'CLOCK.

"This is the first chance I have had since the meeting to write. It truly was glorious! Here is a description. When we were all up there, S. read two or three passages about having all our wants supplied. We then were silent for a little while, and then H. said that we wanted this meeting to be a meeting of thanksgiving; and he gave thanks for having been enabled to consecrate himself *wholly*. I gave thanks for the same thing, and S. did also. Then we kneeled down and C. prayed. S. gave thanks on his knees for entire consecration, and R. prayed for it. I was blessed and filled to overflowing.

"But, my dear mother, I must not write any more, as this is nearly eight pages. Pray, and ask the girls to pray, that we four may be kept full and kept resting.

"Adieu, with much love to all, I remain as I always have been, thy very affectionate son,

"FRANK."

In my reply to this precious letter, I wrote:

"I feel inexpressibly thankful, my darling boy, for the Lord's tender and loving dealings with thy soul, and am indeed truly rejoiced that thee has been enabled to give thyself up so completely to thy dear Saviour. Now, darling Frank, thee will be a happy Christian, as well as a useful one; and I am sure thee will continually learn more and more of the simplicity of the life of faith, so as to be able to look away from thyself, and to have thy eyes fixed on Jesus. The soul can never be discouraged that looks at Him, — never! For He is only love, and tenderness, and forgiving mercy. But when we look at ourselves, then there is nothing but discouragement. Do not expect ever to find any good in thyself, for thee never will; and if thee could, it would be a very bad sign. Our goodness, our strength, our everything, in short, is in Jesus. We are poor sinners, and nothing at all, and Jesus Christ is our all in all!

"Father sends his dear love, and says thy precious letter has rejoiced his heart. Darling son, I feel as if I never could be thankful enough for thy early dedication. It is so sweet to be the Lord's altogether, and His only. How perfectly peaceful and free from care we are, when we know that the Lord has taken us into His dear keeping, and that His Arms are round about us and beneath us. Oh ! I feel like singing 'Praise God, from whom all blessings flow ! '

"And now, dear Frank, do not let any sudden failure, if it should come upon thee, make thee feel that the whole thing is spoiled. It often happens, in the beginning of this life of faith, that there are temporary failures, and that the feet do sometimes stumble. But this need not discourage thee. Sanctification is not a thing once done, and done forever ; it is a life, a walk, and if we stumble we can get up again. It is a life of trust, moment by moment; and if for one moment we fail, that is no reason why we should not trust the next moment. But remember, dear Frank, the very moment thee discovers thy failure, to go at once to Jesus, and have it all washed away in His precious blood. For His promise is, 'If we confess our sins, he is faithful and just to forgive us our sins, and to cleanse us from all unrighteousness.' He does both : He forgives, and then He cleanses and makes us just as pure as before ; and He does it at once, as soon as we confess, so that we need not be hindered a moment.

"Farewell, my own precious boy, — doubly precious now that thee belongs wholly to the Lord ! Oh, may He fill thee with all the fulness of God ! "

CHAPTER VII.

FROM this time onward our dear Frank's will was given up to the Lord. There were some variations in his life, and now and then failures in action; but in the very centre of his soul his *will* was from henceforth on the Lord's side, and was never taken back again; and he proved during the remainder of his young life very fully the blessedness of a heart thus given up to the Lord, finding religion's ways to be to him, indeed, ways of pleasantness, and all her paths, paths of peace. By this step of consecration and of faith, our boy had been brought into the place of liberty, where his soul could "dwell at ease," and where, in the truest sense, he inherited all the good things of the earth.

On the 9th he wrote, after having given one of the Bible lessons he had sent for, in their First-day evening class:

"We have just had an exceedingly interesting Bible class. First I read the texts, telling what are the present possessions of the believer, and got each one to make a list, as thee suggested. It was very interesting; but no one would talk. So I began on the believers' names. Then they got to talking, and the fellows said they had never been to so interesting a lesson up there. —— told me the last lesson on the Assurance of Faith interested him very much, and he hoped I 'd continue. So thee sees, thy lessons are doing some good. The privileges of the believer as shown in these texts has set me to thinking a great deal, and I feel more than ever that I *must* be a whole-hearted Christian. For, as I told Minnie in my last letter, there is no use in being half-way; either be one, or the other.

"Would it be wrong for me to study on First-day? I have so much to do, in order to enter another college; and I could study so much then. Be sure and answer this."

My reply to this question was as follows:

"As to studying on First-day, dear Frank, I would not do it. It seems to be a Divine law somehow, that any secular business done on that day does not prosper, and it has been proved beyond question that no one can work at the same things seven days in the week straight on, without losing his health. Lawyers say that they can really accomplish more by working six days, and resting one, than they can by working seven. I think the Heavenly Father has provided that day for us to be able, with an easy conscience and an undivided heart, to read and meditate and be occupied about heavenly things."

Frank was very anxious to get a thorough education, and in a letter, dated April 9th, he wrote:

"I have a great passion and desire for the best education the country affords. I am exceedingly fond of literature, of classics, and of mathematics. If I could have my choice in life, and if I had the ability, nothing could give me greater pleasure than to be a professor, that I might study. I would a thousand times rather read a good piece of literature than a novel, — a thousand times; and for a little while a day I would rather translate Virgil than do either. But, laying all prospect of being a professor aside as impracticable, I do want a good thorough education. And now about the college. I may as well blurt it out. I want to go to ——. Now, don't tear this letter up, but think about it."

In reference to this letter, he says, in his Diary:

"Wrote home; said I want now to go to ——. Said I'd like to be a professor, and said a whole lot of funny things. Wonder what answer I'll get."

When the answer came, he makes another entry:

"Letter from home. Say I can't go to ——, on account of the Unitarian influences. But I can go through Princeton, and then most likely to a German university. That will suit me almost as well as ——."

About this time he wrote to one of his young friends, who had lately been converted:

"I was very glad to hear that thee had become a Christian, and I do sincerely hope that thee will be a better and more faithful one than I have ever been.

Sometimes when I think of my past life, and think what a hypocrite I have been, — how, while to the world outside I have appeared fair enough, within, I have sinned and sinned, as I have no doubt thee has known; when I think of all this, I have wondered how I could have had any hope then of ever being saved. But I know God is rich in mercy, and I believe He has forgiven my past; as for the future, He will keep me.

"It seemed to me that one newly converted has such a splendid chance to save himself from almost all future remorse about any hypocrisy, if he will only *begin* by keeping Christ between himself and temptation as a sort of shield.

"It was last fall that the Lord showed me how wicked I had been, and enabled me to trust Him more fully for the future.

"I suppose thee has heard of our little daily meeting here. There are ten or eleven of us who meet together daily for half an hour, and we have some very blessed times. The Lord is often with us.

"In reference to my past sad experience, I believe it was all, or a great part, brought on by my refusal to confess in public that I was on the Lord's side years ago, when I was at Millville. It was a great drawback to me."

On the 10th of April he writes in his Diary:

"Only day after to-morrow I'll go home for the golden wedding at 'Ivy Lodge.' Hurrah!"

This was the golden wedding of Frank's grandpa and grandma Smith, and was celebrated by a large family gathering in their hospitable home in Shoemakers' Lane, Germantown. It was an occasion of great interest, and dear Frank, as the oldest grandchild and one dearly beloved, was one of the important parties to the celebration.

He writes in his Diary concerning it:

"*April* 12, 1871. The golden-wedding day! Had a grand time at the wedding. Waited on N. It was jolly. At last we got together alone, and had a first-rate private talk about our experiences. She told me all about herself, and I about myself, religiously. It was very interesting."

A short time after, he wrote to his beloved aunt, E. P. S.:

"DARLING AUNTY:

"Obediently to my promise, I sit down to write to thee. I feel very hot and very lazy, and out of six letters I wanted to write to-day, this one is the third and the last. The other two were to father and mother; so thee sees that next to them you all rank very high in my affections, for I can tell thee I only write to the people I love best. Really I have come to consider 'Ivy Lodge' as a sort of second home to me, where I always find a welcome, and always find people I love dearly. I 'm not of a very expressive nature, but you must remember that 'still waters run deep.' . . . .

"And now for my experience. It is almost too deep to tell. A will entirely surrendered; a faith given me by Christ; a constant rest and peace in

Him, comprises nearly all of it. Only so blessed, so entirely different from anything I ever experienced before, that it seems like a separate life from the old one. If Christians only could realize the perfect rest there is in Christ, they would be compelled to leave their *trying* to be good all in His hands.

"My feelings, too, are somewhat changed. I used to dislike some of the fellows so much, as thee knows, and now I fairly love them. I used to be considerably vexed at one or two in our little meeting, who never spoke, because I thought they were doing us harm in keeping us back. But now the Lord has taken all that away, and I feel just as full of love, and just as united in spirit to them, as if they had spoken.

"But I am still very weak; and have to remind myself continually that I am not living this life myself, that I have not changed myself; but that Christ is living in me, and that Christ has changed me. I feel just like a monument of what Christ can do for an unwilling disciple.

"But I have talked too much about myself. We have very blessed meetings now; we have them in the morning before breakfast, and to me they are very sweet. M. and C. H. seem both to have entered into this life of rest too. Isn't it a cause for thankfulness?

"But, dear auntie, it is bedtime. Give ever so much love to grandpa and grandma, and remember that when I say I love thee, I mean it.

"Affectionately, thy 'nevvy,'

"F. W. SMITH."

On April 25th, he wrote in his Diary: "I feel so joyful in the Lord to-day. It is continually easier for me to walk in Him."

And a few days later:

"I have surrendered myself wholly to Christ, and He keeps me wonderfully. I really believe He does guide me. I hope I do just as He tells me up in our meetings. I do not want to do anything in my own strength, but only His will."

On April 30th, he wrote to me:

"DARLING MOTHER:

"C. H. and I walked down to Hestonville yesterday, to see Uncle Horry and Aunt Maggie. We had a splendid walk; told each other our experiences and difficulties, our prospects in life, and what we had to give up, and so on. Our experiences are very much the same, an entire surrender to Christ, a constant watch over ourselves to see that we take nothing back from the consecration; and a constant belief that God will keep us abiding in Him. We have our dark seasons, when our trials are very great, when it seems almost impossible to keep trusting Christ; but those I spend in constant prayer, and I am helped through them. I am really wonderfully guided by the Holy Spirit, because I have His promise that He will guide me, and I believe it. I never have any difficulty in knowing His will; and although I do not follow it as I ought to, yet each day it gets easier. I had no idea of the rest of this life. Every time I feel troubled about myself, I go right to the Lord, and He removes it."

The C. H. spoken of in this letter was Frank's cousin and dearest friend. Their intimacy continued unchanged until our dear boy was taken away, and was always a joy and a strength to them both. Drawn together by the sweet bond of Christian fellowship, they became far more to each other than merely common friends.

It has been a great loss to us that most of the letters written by our boy to this dearly loved friend have been destroyed, C. H. having made a change of residence, and having dreamed of nothing but a lifelong intimacy between them. But their intercourse was always on the basis of Christian faith and experience, which, while drawing them continually nearer to each other, drew them nearer to Christ also. Often in his Pocket-diary there are such entries as this: "Talked with Charlie until two o'clock last night." "Charlie sick; took care of him Tuesday and Wednesday nights. Talked till about one or two." "Had a jolly walk and talk with C. H."

And Charlie, in writing to us since Frank's death, says:

"I cannot express to you better how I feel his loss, than to tell you that he was the only person who filled the place of a twin brother to me; for although our ages differed a year or two, we were both baptized into the fulness of the Gospel at the same time, and we did truly enjoy a fellowship in Christ.

"This was the secret of our love for each other; and while we enjoyed the pleasures of this life together, whenever we settled down to a good long talk, we never, as far as I can remember, forgot that we were in His hands."

On the 6th of May, 1871, we had our last "Hestonville party," at Uncle Horry's; and Frank thus notices it in his Diary:

"We did have just a jolly time at Hestonville to-day. Formed into a society, and decided to write a history. Agreed each one of us to write once a year to the Corresponding Secretary; and to have a grand reunion on the Fourth of July, 1876. Jolly fun. This is the last Hestonville. I could almost cry."

And on the 7th he wrote home to me concerning it:

"I think we had an elegant time yesterday. That 'Society' was a perfect success. All our plans, which I suppose the girls have told thee, exactly suit me. Will thee have time to compile our history? I guess thee will. Thee *must*. What does thee think about our reunion in 1876? Won't it be fun? And the idea of having a corresponding secretary, to keep accounts of our doings, is just grand. I would not mind having Charlie's place one bit myself."

After a little more about this, and planning for a picnic in the summer, dear Frank goes on, in the same letter, to what he calls his "weekly report" of his experience. A precious report, that it was our happy privilege to receive from our boy every few days, during all the rest of his life. He writes:

"As for my weekly report: Charlie, I believe, is still trusting and happy. But for myself, I hardly know what to say. I do trust the Lord to keep me, and He does it, a great deal. But it seems somehow I can't trust Him enough; I mean, that, when I am thinking of Him, I am able to trust Him fully; but before I know it I forget Him, and then a temptation comes suddenly, and I fail. Of course, He always enables me to stop short, whatever it may be, and confess it, and then He does forgive me. But I'd rather be kept entirely. Is it not His way to keep us entirely? Of course, if this is only to be attained by a gradual growth, I am willing to wait; but I thought it came at first. Besides, although I feel tolerably restful, yet I am not at all happy. Pray that my experience may become deeper.

"We had the lesson on the Passover, this evening, in the Bible class. It was very interesting to me, and did me a great deal of good in showing me how entirely dependent we are on the blood of Christ, — more so than on our faith, or anything else. It is a great trial to my faith to find myself in my present barren condition; but I can truly say, as I am writing to thee, that I believe in the Lord's own good time, He will give me joy in Him. I only hope it will be soon.

"Give Mary lots of love, and tell her I've got the shrubs yet she gave me at Hestonville, and also the taste of the sweet kiss she gave me just as we were running off. Give love to all the rest of the 'chicks.'"

From this letter it will be seen that dear Frank was experiencing the sort of reaction that often follows seasons of great joy in the Christian life, and that, not having learned fully the lesson of walking by faith, he had become discouraged by it. In my reply I said:

"As to thy Christian experience, dear boy, I do not think thee need be at all discouraged. The life of faith is, in one sense, a growth; that is, the *habit* of trusting grows, until it becomes as it were a second nature, and we trust, almost as we breathe, without being definitely conscious of it. But in the beginning of this life, the usual experience is apt to be such as thee describes, rather variable and sometimes failing. But thee has learned the *secret;* and if thee always goes back at once, upon the discovery of thy failure, to the blood of Christ for forgiveness and cleansing, thee will find thy soul so getting into the habit of looking to the Lord Jesus and His cleansing blood, as to wander no more. I do not think a perfect and complete victory always comes just at first. It is like a child learning to walk; it may have many a tumble at first. But if it is not discouraged by its tumbles, but just jumps up and goes ahead, it will be able to walk after a while without falling. If, however, its falls discourage it, and it gives up in despair, it will never walk at all. Just go on as thee is doing, my darling boy, trusting as fully as possible; and when thee fails, at once confess thy failure to the Lord, and believe in the forgiveness and the cleansing that He has promised in 1 John i. 9, and all will be well.

"As for joy, dear Frank, thy joy is to be *in the Lord,* not in thyself. Spiritual joy is not a thing, not a lump of joy, so to speak, stored away in your heart, to be looked at and rejoiced over. Our joy is all in Christ. We rejoice that we have Him for our Saviour; we rejoice in His love and in His power to save. I suffered a great deal from just this — that I looked for and expected to have joy as a thing by itself; and I never found it, and that discouraged me. But now I never think whether I have joy or not. I have Christ, and that is enough. I am *glad* that I have Him, and this gladness I do believe is the true sort of Christian joy. It is surely something to be glad about, to know that we have such a Saviour and such a salvation. So, dear Frank, give up looking for joy, and just take all the comfort thee can out of the gifts the Lord has already given thee, and be glad of thy salvation, and rejoice in Christ. Does thee understand the distinction between rejoicing in thy joy and rejoicing in Christ?

"I expect thy present state of mind is just as the Lord would have it to be. If thee is conscious of being entirely given up to Him, it must be; because where He has his way with us, He will make us right. And yet this may not always be manifest to us. A lump of clay that is in the process of transformation to be made into a beautiful vase, has to go through many different stages; and the earlier stages may not be perhaps at all beautiful or attractive. But the Potter knows what He is about, and the lump of clay must be content to be just as *He* would have it, and not as it would like to be itself. Thee is that lump of clay, my darling boy, and thy only concern need be to *let* the Heavenly Potter have His own way with thee. He will surely then make out of thee a 'vessel unto honor, sanctified and meet for the Master's use, and fitted to every good work.'

"Farewell, my own precious darling boy! How I do love thee, and what a comfort thee is to me!

"Thy own mother, H. W. S."

In a letter to his father, in this month of May, Frank says:

"The question of work is one that has occupied me a great deal lately. Christ has done so much for me, has spent so much love and tender compassion on me, that I can never bear to think of how little I am doing for Him. How I wish I had more faith to trust Him to guide me in this matter! My way in the College seems a good deal shut up, as I cannot very well speak to any of the upper classes, and nearly all my own class are Christians. Those who are not, I have talked to so often, that they don't care to hear me. I hope to try, trusting in the Lord for strength, tract-distributing around the country when I am out walking. Perhaps I can do something for Him in this way. Of course, we can only do a *very* little towards repaying our debt of gratitude to Christ; but the mite we can do I want to do with all my heart; and I want to enter into this work in His strength, and not in my own in the least. There was a time when the very thought of becoming a preacher, even like thee, was excessively repugnant to me; but now there is nothing I should consider more joyful than to be gifted by Jesus to proclaim His gospel. It would be glorious!

"Perhaps thee never knew it, but my air-castle

has always been to become a thoroughly honest and upright lawyer; to work my way up gradually until I should become a prominent Christian statesman, upholding the right. It may sound foolish to thee, but I suppose it is the same thought and ambition nearly every young fellow has; and I used to think that to give up this, and settle down into a simple preacher of the gospel, would be dreadful. But now I can see that the call, 'Feed my sheep,' is far higher than any earthly ambition. After all, what does fame amount to in this world? A mere thing of time, a simple bubble, when compared to the 'Well done, thou good and faithful servant; enter thou into the joy of thy Lord,' which lasts forever. Oh, how blessed it would be to do something for Him!"

From this letter it will be seen that Frank had begun to feel, as every soul truly at rest in the Lord must necessarily feel, a longing desire to work for his Master. Having a heart now "at leisure from itself," he was able to go out in yearning after others, and in his quiet, gentle way he tried to tell one and another the sweet story of the love of Jesus, and to win them to give themselves to Him. One of his companions, not himself a Christian, writing to us, says:

"I feel it my privilege, as one who knew dear Frank well, and who watched him through the very trying ordeal of college-life, to testify to his consistent Christian walk and conversation, and to his constant endeavor, both in word and example, to work for the glory and honor of his Divine Master and the eternal welfare of his classmates. Many a time has he pleaded earnestly with me, as a true friend should, to fix my attention on things above.

"I consider it far harder to make a pretence before your companions in college than anywhere else; in fact, it can't be done. And all who knew Frank at Haverford would join with me in saying that his influence had always been for good."

In a letter written in the early part of May, Frank thus refers to an effort he had made for one of his friends, which resulted in great blessing.

"To my great surprise, —— told me yesterday, when I spoke to him about it, that he had not yet entered into that full rest I thought he had. So I prayed for him, and prayed that I might be guided how to speak to him. And at last he gave up his unbelief, and this morning, in our little meeting, he confessed it, and said the Lord had kept him wonderfully. A cause for praise, is it not?"

This young man has sent us the following account of this circumstance, and of his intercourse with our dear boy while at Haverford and afterward. He writes:

"I scarcely know where to begin in writing about dear Frank. Our acquaintance really began at Haverford, though we had known each other from childhood. Our brotherhood, at all events, began there.

"When Frank came to Haverford, he found very little religious life among the students, even those who were Christians. Although not then in the

Higher Life, he mourned over this in himself and others, and induced his father to come out and hold a series of meetings with some of us; and memorable meetings they were in the history of our lives.

"Then we commenced holding daily prayer-meetings among ourselves, in which Frank's voice was often heard in prayer and faithful testimony. And, looking back at that eventful winter in the light of the last few months, it seems as if we could mark his growth in grace, so rapid and manifest was it about that time.

"In the spring of 1871, I was called away from the College for about three weeks, by ill-health. During this time, Frank and two others, C. H. and C. S., had a wonderful meeting together, at which time, I believe, they all felt that they had entered upon the 'Highway of Holiness.' When I returned to the College I was struck with the change in Frank. His spirit seemed to have grown so restful, while his love for Christ and for his fellow-students was even more ardent than before. He took a warm interest in me from that time, as I seemed to have been left behind the rest of them. We were often together, and he used to try and make the way of faith plain to me; but I thought it contrary to reason, and, consequently, would not accept it.

"On one occasion, about the 1st of May, we took a long walk together, and Frank compared the restful state of his heart to my own unsatisfied hungry condition, and pressed upon me the claims of the Saviour for the possession of my whole heart, — till I could stand it no longer, and proposed that we should kneel down together by the roadside, under a tree, while I gave myself up to the Lord. I shall never forget the spot, nor the joyful look with which he assented. But little was said as we returned to the College; we were both too full of our own feelings.

"Next morning, when we met at our little prayer-meeting, I said to him, 'It bears,' alluding to the experience of the day before. 'Of course it does!' he replied, with emphasis.

"Soon after this, a few of us had an especial little meeting to pray for the baptism of the Holy Spirit. Dear Frank's prayer on this occasion was very sweet; in fact, his prayers were always different from anybody else's at Haverford. They were perfectly natural. He asked for just what he wanted; his tone was conversational, if I may so speak; it seemed as if he were really holding communion with the Lord; and the general directness and simplicity of his manner was strongly in contrast with the strained, difficult way in which so many young believers are apt to pray.

"Naturally reserved and quiet, he rarely spoke at any length in our meetings, but what he said carried power with it, and especially his prayers.

"Soon after this time, about the middle of May, we two read together 'Holiness through Faith,' written by Frank's father, and some of dear Frank's comments and prayers in connection with different parts were especially beautiful.

"After Commencement I saw but little of him during the summer. He was at Newport for a few weeks, and I took one or two sails with him. He was a grand swimmer, and saved a classmate's life once at Haverford while bathing in the Schuylkill. The student himself told me this. I never heard Frank allude to it.

"In the spring of 1872, I spent one night with him at 1315 Filbert street. Before going to sleep, I recounted to him all my hindrances and troubles, and he confessed to having some of them himself, and especially to what he termed 'deadness or want of feeling on the subject.' (I must say that I never noticed anything of the kind in him.) He said that this was in the way of his work at Princeton; and together that night we besought the Lord for help and strength. Dear Frank's prayer on this occasion was particularly submissive and sweet. He expressed his confidence in the Lord's word, and that we were in the right way, and then added, 'And we know that thou wilt give us feeling, when it is right for us to have it, and when we can bear it.' After this we talked of the forgiveness of sins, and the fear of death, and Frank said he believed that fear had been entirely removed from him, and he was not afraid to die.

"The next morning, in one of the early morning meetings held in his father's parlor during the week of the Friends' Yearly Meeting, he spoke very sweetly, testifying to the peace of a full surrender to Christ. This was the last time we ever met on earth. The next time, I trust, will be beside the river of Life, in the Heaven we so loved to talk of."

CHAPTER VIII.

ON the 14th of May, Frank wrote to me :

. . . .

"—— and I go together a great deal now. He is one of the most manly fellows in the College. Everybody respects and likes him. Now tell me, is this the right condition for a Christian, — to be honored and respected as he is? Or ought he to be fairly despised, and rejected, and spurned? That question has been troubling me a good deal lately. The Bible most assuredly says, Christ was 'despised and rejected of men,' and we are to bear His yoke. But then it also says that a Christian shall be blessed even in this world. What are you to do? Fairly *seek* unpopularity, as some I know do, because they think it right; or — well, I suppose just let it alone, as to seek popularity is most certainly wrong. Then, here is another question about it. If you are very popular, you can exert a great influence for the right; whereas, if you are unpopular, everything you do works against the cause. Oh, dear, dear, such a question is hard to decide.

"Another thing. Often, in my walking, I go with

fellows who don't care a cent for the rules. Well now, for instance, we walk in the evening, and we come to the limits of the bounds; and there I have to stop and say, I cannot go outside, because it is against the rules. Immediately, I have no doubt, the fellows think I am setting myself up to be better than they; think I am sanctimonious, and all that. I hate to be thought of in that way, above all things.

"What does Eph. v. 4 mean? That we are never to talk foolishly or jestingly at all? That would make us dreadfully sombre and morose. I cannot believe that is what Christ wants. It seems to me if we only pray at the time for help, and trust for it, we will have it; at least, I have found it so.

"What thee told me about not being discouraged by a few falls, helped me a good deal, for I was getting a little discouraged. I think I can trust now. . . .

"Suppose thee sends out some tracts for the unconverted next week, so that when I go walking I can give them to the people I meet. I do so want to do some work, little as it may be."

In answer to Frank's question about popularity, I wrote him:

"Thee solves the question thyself, dear Frank, when thee says, 'just let it alone.' That is it. Do not seek popularity or unpopularity, but simply have a single eye to Jesus, and let Him take the care of thy reputation into His own hands; and remember, it is one thing to be hated for Christ's sake, and quite a different thing to be hated because of being disagreeable. The Lord Jesus was rejected and despised because of His mission, and not because of anything disagreeable in Him; and He is our example.

"Eph. v. 4 does not mean that innocent playfulness, which is, I think, perfectly legitimate for young people. The very best Christians I know, are the happiest and the merriest. Those who have entered into this blessed experience of abiding in Christ are light-hearted and fairly gay; they can afford to be natural, because they have given their natures up into the control of the Lord, and He regulates them aright. It is only the half-hearted Christians who have to be constrained and walk on stilts. As a child, whose heart is entirely set to be obedient to its parents, can go on at perfect ease and naturally until the parent tells it to change its course, so we may leave all responsibility as to our lives in the Lord's hands, and go on at ease and naturally, unless He speaks and calls for a change of course. The branch is not all the while making an effort to *produce* fruit; it simply *bears* it, and leaves to the husbandman all the labor of cultivation, and of making it productive. And we are nothing but the branches, Christ is the Vine, and our Father is the Husbandman! Surely, we can afford to leave ourselves to His care!

"I love to think of thee, my precious boy, in the care of thy dear Lord; His arms around thee, and His love enfolding thee!"

To his "Aunty Lill" Frank wrote about this time:

"Ever so dear Auntie:

"I was very glad, indeed, to get thy letter week before last. It was very encouraging to me to find thee was so glad of my being able to trust Christ, although I knew thee would be. It truly is a blessed life. But my faith is weak. It seems hard to keep *continually* trusting. I am so apt to forget for a moment, and then immediately I fall. But, as mother says, I know I must not be discouraged by my falls; only let them make me more anxious to return. As long as I am enabled to abide, it is a far greater and deeper joy than any the world gives. Tell grandpa I do realize the Christian's life to be a joyous one. I always used to think that when I should become an entirely consecrated Christian, I would have to be sombre and morose, and live altogether separated from the world. But I have seen how often we are exhorted to rejoice and be joyful; and have noticed that text in John, 'I pray not that thou shouldst take them out of the world, but that thou shouldst keep them from the evil.' There is our distinction, it seems to me, — that we should join heartily with this world's pleasure, so long as we can take Christ there with us, and can do it with a perfectly good conscience."

With all his deep interest in the glorious salvation he had learned so fully to rejoice in, Frank did not lose his enjoyment of the college games, but entered into them with hearty energy, and a determination, if possible, to excel. On May 11th, he wrote in his little diary:

"Played on cricket-crease, and made one run on an underhand ball! I guess I'm the best player here, only the fellows don't know it!!! Was bowled out on a swift round arm of P. E. Nasty shooter, that I can never manage."

And again: "We played a match with G., etc. We beat by one run; score 32 and 33. I made ten runs!"

To his father he writes: "I find myself considerably behindhand on the cricket-field, but play all the spare time I have, and perhaps I can learn by the time I am a Senior. They say there is a great deal of science in cricket, and that six years hard practice is scarcely enough to make a really good player."

On the 18th of May, he writes in his diary: "Accepted the offer to speak before the Loganian Society, on July 11th. Whew!"

On the 21st, he writes: "Wrote home to B. and to father. Twelve pages to mother. Poor woman! I pity her, for she 's got to read it!"

But it was not a letter any mother need be pitied for receiving — a precious letter, telling me all his life, both inward and outward, as he always did, perfectly sure of my loving sympathy in everything.

"Darling Mother:

"I have lots to tell, and to say to thee to-day, so do not be surprised if the letter is a little long. In the first place, I am *very* much obliged for the basket. Its contents thee may believe were mighty acceptable, especially the strawberries, which were the first that have been out here. I would wish thee encouraged, if it is not asking too much.

"And now comes a piece of news, the greatest I have had to tell thee for a long while. I was walking through the study-room, the other day, when a

Senior and a Junior called to me, and said, 'Smith, you have been appointed to make an original declamation before the Loganian Society, the night before Commencement.' They said it was a great honor for a Freshman to have it; and wanted to know if I would accept it. I said I would think about it. And so I prayed it over, and asked God to show me what was right. I told Him I would like to glorify Him in it, and asked Him for help in writing it. Well, I slept over it, and the next morning I came to the conclusion it was right; that it would be a splendid chance for self-improvement, and that I could really glorify God by it. So I have accepted it; and now, of course, I want to do my very best. I have to choose my own subject, and, as usual, I come to thee."

He then gave me a little sketch of the subject he proposed taking, and, after touching on other matters, continued:

"Our morning Bible-classes are gradually bringing us out. We are studying 1 John through, and yesterday came to the text, 'Love not the world,' etc., when one of the class took it literally, thinking it referred to God's actual outward creation, and that we were not to love the beauty we see there. Of course we all came out at that, and said we thought it brought us nearer to God, to love what He has created. I know it is one of my especial delights to look at and admire nature, and then realize that the same God who made all things for us 'richly to enjoy;' the same God who guides and governs them all, loves me individually, with such a tender, compassionate, forgiving love, and so great a love too. I feel like doing nothing but work for Him all my life.

"Another idea was advanced, that we were to have nothing to do with the world in any way, except to preach to them; that we ought not even to play cricket with an unconverted fellow, because it brings us into company that is not directly Christian in its influences. What does thee think? And still another idea was, that we must never, in all our lives, be five minutes in company with any unconverted person, of our own age or otherwise, a stranger or a friend, without saying something about Christ. It seems to me, for fellows of our age, young and inexperienced as we are, this would be taking a good deal on ourselves. Tell me what thee thinks.

"I am very much obliged for thy answers about popularity, etc., and about Eph. v. 4. They are very satisfactory to my mind, and encouraging. I am afraid I have been seeking popularity too much, and it has made me unhappy."

In answer to Frank's questions in this letter, I wrote:

"It seems to me that text, 'He giveth us richly *all things* to enjoy,' answers one of the difficulties thee mentions. God made the world for our use, and comfort, and pleasure, and I think it would be ungrateful in us not to enjoy it. And as to the other idea, that we are to have nothing to do with the unconverted, there is a full answer to be found, I think, in the directions about going to feasts in 1 Cor.

x. 27; and Paul's words, in 1 Cor. v. 9–11, that if we did thus separate ourselves, 'we must needs go out of the world;' taken with what our Saviour prayed for us, —not that we should be taken out of the world, but kept from the evil that is in it.

"As to speaking to every one about their soul—that is dreadful legality! The Lord don't want us to make any such rules for ourselves; He wants to guide us Himself by His blessed Spirit; and if we commit it to Him, He will show us when and where and to whom to speak; and then he always makes it easy. For when He leads His own sheep out, He *goeth before* them, and makes a way for them."

To one of his cousins, to whom Frank was much attached, and who, like himself, had been much helped by the religious communion and fellowship enjoyed at their Hestonville parties, he thus writes:

"Dear ——:

"I have been wanting to write to thee ever since Yearly Meeting week, but have not had time.

"I was real sorry thee was not out at Hestonville when we last went. We had a jolly time. Of course, thee knows all about the H. V. P. Society and its proposed doings. Won't it be fun to meet together in 1876? And as for the prospect of our picnic,—it seems almost too good to be true.

"What fun we have had at Hestonville! I should think thee would miss the girls very much, now thee is out in the country. How does thee do without them? And then the little meetings—thee must miss them like everything. Just think what we were this time last year; or, at least, I 'll speak for myself. Christians, I have no doubt, but so cold, heartless, and dead, that we would not have worked for Christ in any way, nor have spoken in a meeting for all the world. And now what a change! Although, for my part, I am still far from what I ought to be, yet I know Christ has filled us both with so much love for Him, and so much power in Him, that we would be willing to do anything for His sake. How far superior this is to the old life, in happiness and everything else!

"And, dear ——, what a responsible position we hold among our cousins. Just think, we two are the only ones among them who profess to be given up to Christ! And how we shall have to hold up the standard of holiness, and show them that our life is a really happy one. Do let us pray earnestly for —— and ——. If they could only be made real hearty Christians, what splendid times we 'd have this summer. For, after all, I do not know of any subject I am so much interested in as Christ.

"But my paper is at an end. Do write soon to me. I will write every other week, if thee will. And so fare thee well, my very dear cousin; and believe me when I say I do love thee very much, though I never have expressed it.

"Thine for life, etc.,

"FRANK W. SMITH."

CHAPTER IX.

N the 28th, Frank wrote to his father, who was away from home:

"Darling Father:

"It seems very strange to think of thee away out at San Francisco. What a comfort it is to know that one's dearest friends are in the Lord's keeping. It never occurs to me to be afraid for thee, because I know our Father will not let anything happen that is not perfectly right and according to His will. I am very much obliged for 'The Victory of the Vanquished.' It is very interesting and stirring, and brings Christ's life somehow very near to one. I liked it very much, indeed. How differently Christ's love reveals itself to different people. To me it comes wonderfully and sweetly through nature; each proof of His Almighty power seems to me but a new proof of His Almighty love in two ways. First, in giving us richly 'all things to enjoy;' and, second, in showing how great the condescension and love must have been to descend to us.

"Oh, father, since reading this book, Christ has

revealed himself to me so wonderfully as being the ideal of perfection, I have always had, embodied. And that ideal dwelling in me, — to think of it, — ignorant, weak, failing me! That I, who have displeased Him so all my life, should now have Christ living in me, guiding my every-day actions, no matter how small and insignificant, does seem too wonderful almost to be true.

"I have something for which I want thee to pray for me. I have an original oration before the Loganian Society the evening before Commencement. Please pray that I may be helped to write it, so as to glorify God in it.

"It is not worth while to ask thee whether thee is prospering, because I pray for it every night, and know the prayer is answered.

"Very lovingly, thy son,

"FRANK."

On the 31st he wrote to his Aunt E.:

"MY VERY DEAR AUNTIE:

"I would have written to thee three days ago, but I was attacked with an aggravated form of 'spring fever,' and it was so hot, that I absolutely could not do anything but go out of doors and lie in my hammock. Besides, I was deep in the 'Victory of the Vanquished,' by the author of the 'Schönberg Cotta Family.' Has thee read it? It brings a part of Christ's life most beautifully before one, I think. Somehow it seemed to bring the reality of His sufferings for us, and His love towards us, very near to me. And I have realized in a more full sense than ever before what Christ was, or I should rather say, is to me. It does seem so wonderful that Christ, who is perfect holiness and strength, and all, embodied, dwells within us continually, as long as we only trust Him. And that His indwelling does not make us sombre or morose, but entirely the opposite; in fact, making our very countenances beam with joy."

On the 29th, Frank wrote in his Diary:

"G. P. was up in our Bible-class, and gave us a few encouraging words to keep on in the 'good fight.' Our privileges, and therefore responsibilities, are very great. The fellows went on a 'row' to-night, singing down the turnpike, and all around. Well, I tell you I was tempted to go, but was enabled to be kept from it."

On the 7th of June he wrote:

"At home with weak eyes. Caulked boat. Began Essay. Kind of lazy work, lounging around home. Plenty of cherries and strawberries. Had a splendid talk with mother, by which I was convinced I was not allowing myself enough happiness in my Christian life."

After his return to College, he wrote to me:

"I tell thee, mother, thy talk to me that night did me heaps of good. I'm not afraid to be happy now, as I was before. And Christ seems so much nearer to me than ever before; right with me, somehow. I like to regard Christ with the same kind of love I imagine I should have if I were in love with a young lady, only ten thousand times greater. What would I not do for her sake? And far more, therefore, what won't I do for Christ's sake? The highest ambition I have now is to work for my Saviour. It seems to me that I have a revelation of His love, such as no one ever had before. Of course it is not so, because I am no more favored than any one else; only it seems so. But I cannot put my feelings on paper somehow. It is because they are too deep for expression."

In answer to this, I wrote to Frank:

"Thy experience, my precious boy, is very blessed. I thank the Lord with all my heart for His great mercies to thee. This revelation of the love of Christ which has been granted to thee, gives thee a little foretaste of what it will be to pass an eternity with Jesus; and it has also taught thee how it is possible to be in ourselves poor sinners and nothing at all, but to find Him to be our all in all. It is a blessed thing to have such revelations of Christ; it is infinitely more glorious than any amount of telling about it by another! Does thee not find that thee *knows* now what before thee only imagined, or rather imagined could not be? But do not expect, dear boy, ever to find thy old nature any better or any nearer thy ideal; for thee never, never will. Thee thyself, that is, thy old nature, will always be utterly vile, and ignorant, and corrupt; but Jesus is thy life now. It is with thee, 'no more I,' but Christ who liveth in thee. And is not this glorious — to lose thy own life, and find Christ's divine life put in its place? To cease to be of the race of the first Adam, and to become one of the race of the second Adam, the Lord from heaven! It is far more glorious than it would be for an animal to cease to be an animal and to be transformed into a man. Never look into thy own heart then for any sort of satisfaction or comfort. Thee will never find any goodness there, — no stocks of virtue laid up to draw upon. But thy goodness is all *in Christ*, and thee must draw it from Him moment by moment as thee needs it. Andrew Longacre says that some Christians are so thrifty, that they do not like to live 'from hand to mouth,' as the saying is, but want to have a stock of goodness laid up ahead, and a stock of wisdom, and of patience, and of all the other graces. But he says God's plan for us is different. He has laid it all up for us in Christ, and we have to draw it each moment as we need it. If thee feels thyself then to be in thyself mean, and foolish, and altogether vile, just look at Christ, and say to thyself, 'Never mind, all I need is there ready for me, whenever I have occasion to use it; and having Christ, I have all things.' Our view of our own vileness, therefore, need not discourage us. Of course, *we* are vile, but our life is in Christ, — He is our life! I can, with untold joy, thank God for thee, my own precious boy.

"This is such a simple and child-like way of living, that many Christians overlook it altogether, and weary themselves out in trying to reach up to some great height when what they really need is to sink down into Christ. Some old writer says that 'God's will is a pillow to rest on, and not a load to carry;' but this is only true to the soul that is altogether given up to Him."

On the 16th, Frank wrote to his father:

"DEAR DARLING FATHER:

"I have not written to thee for ever so long, and the only excuse I have is because I was at home with weak eyes. It was not because I do not love thee, for there is not an hour passes hardly, but I think of and pray for thee. Oh, how often I pray that God will give me the power thee has in speaking to people! There is nothing I covet so much, no earthly accomplishment or acquirement. Only let me work for my Master, and see His marks of approval on my work, as thee does, and I ask no more. But I remember for the present that I must not expect too much, as I am so young, and even Jesus did not preach till He was thirty. I really believe I am ready to do any work for Him though, that He may call me to at present.

"Well, father, I *never* had any idea of the blessedness of a consecrated life before I tried it. The peace, the rest, and the joy I have whenever I think of whose I am, and of how entirely I am His, is absolutely beyond the power of my pen to express. I never enjoyed the innocent pleasures of this life half so much; and, to tell the whole truth, I never had anything like so great liberty in doing what I please, simply because I have no desire to do anything my precious, precious Saviour would not like. Fellows come to me and ask me to do wrong things that used to be very attractive to me, but now absolutely I do not care for them. Such freedom from bondage never appeared possible to me before; and yet I don't mean to say I have no temptations, because I have; but the Lord gives me a surety of victory, and I meet them with joy, in the certainty of another conquest. However, thee knows this life better than I do, and I suppose it is nothing new; but it seems to me that no one could ever have realized it as I do.

"And, oh, father! I never loved thee and mother nearly so much as I do now. It seems to add a new zest to my love, and to make a bond unspeakably precious between us. I said in one of my letters that I was not where I wanted to be; and I have since found out that the true reason was because I was afraid to be happy. But mother got me out of that at home, and now I realize that Christ means me to be just as happy as I can possibly be; and that not only religiously, although that is the most blessed part, but temporally also, here with the pleasures of this earth. All that will give me true happiness and leave no sting behind, He will grant me.

"How I have to thank the Lord for such parents as I have. Where would I be, if I was ——'s son, for instance? But, father dear, as it is Private Review now, and hard studying, I shall have to close this dear little talk with thee.

"Very lovingly, thy consecrated son,

"FRANK."

In reply to this, Frank's father wrote:

"DEAR FRESHMAN:

"Thy letter is most welcome. We sent off a box of grapes by to-day's Express, which be careful not to leave unopened too long.

"I am so glad to hear that thee is trusting fully in the Lord. It is such a restful, solid position, and has before it the untold treasuries of grace all open. Let us, dear son, be *millionaires in grace,* — accepting, without measure, the gifts of God.

"I hope much from thee, not only in open confession among thy fellow-students, but also from the undesigned hourly influence of thy character, which, it is a solemn fact, tells more on those around us than even our preaching. So that our aim should be primarily to *be,* rather than to *act,* and then let the acting come out spontaneously. See to it that thy character is Christ living in thee, and all will fall into harmony.

"I believe that in days of prosperity and joy there is an especial sweetness in such a full surrender to and trust in Jesus. Oh, how lovely to do this as a thank-offering in the joyfulness of prosperity — not to have to be led to it through sorrow!

"I hope to see thee Friday of next week on my way home, and hope to find thee happier than ever in the Lord; and in the sense of His favor enjoying all the innocent pleasures around thee. Above all I trust I shall find thee happy in the consciousness of walking 'in the will of God,' and not outside of it.

"Thy loving and praying father,

"R. P. S."

On the 22d of June, he wrote to one of his cousins as follows:

"DEAR B——:

"Is thee coming in to see the graduating class at C. M. S.'s School next week? Charlie and I are going to send three bouquets to the three young ladies. But would it not be a joke, if I should not get any invitation?

"I had quite an adventure yesterday. It happened thuswise: There were five of us Freshmen over swimming at the Schuylkill, where it is about a quarter of a mile wide; we had all swum across, and A. and I., having swum back again, had got out and were partly dressed; we were talking quietly on the bank, and watching the other fellows swimming back, when suddenly from the middle of the river came the cry, 'Cramp, I've got the cramp!' I looked, and there was C., with his head just above water, calling for help. I called to the fellows who had just got in shore to go out for him, but they were too tired; and then came the cry again, 'Quick, Frank, I've got the cramp!' Well, in less time than I can tell it, I had my clothes off, and jumping right into the water, I swam for him as hard as I could. There he was in the middle of the river, as quiet as he could be, every now and then going under above his mouth and nose, and I saw he could not hold out much longer. So I just prayed that I might be helped to save him, and I felt sure of an answer. Then I swam with all my might, and I believe I never swam so fast in my life; and I got there just as he was about to give up. He put his hand on my shoulder, and I got him half-way in, when the other fellows met us with a log. But I tell thee, he was near under; his face was getting blue a little, and he says in about five seconds more he would have gone under. My! but I was thankful to my Heavenly Father for helping me, because without His help I might not have done it; C. might have got frightened, and pulled me under, for instance. But it is all right now.

"And here I have written a letter exclusively about myself. Please answer in a similar strain.

"Thy loving cousin, FRANK."

Except to this cousin, our dear boy scarcely spoke of the adventure — as he calls it — related above. To us it seems like an act of real Christian heroism; but to him it seemed something so simple and natural as to be worth very little thought, and even his father did not know of it until after his death.

His last letter to his father from Haverford was written on the 25th of June. In it he says:

"As to my experience, I think thee knows it all. Almost the same. An unclouded brightness and blessing of love as long as I look at Christ; but whenever I look away, no matter for how short a time, utter misery. It is joy to me to read the Bible, and to think of Christ all the time; but sometimes when I forget it, or rather feel too lazy, which I am sorry to say sometimes happens, I get so extremely wretched, that I not only lose all interest in the things of Heaven, but even in the fun going on around me, until I return. As far as I know, I am

Christ's completely, and have no wish but to follow Him."

On the 9th of July he wrote to his Aunt E.:

"DEAREST AUNTIE:

"We have been examined in five out of our six books, and the last one I do not feel much afraid of, so I have a little time to write to thee. I sent thee one of the programmes for next Third-day, with a request that thee would not come. Please don't. Thee knows I should like to see thee very much, but I do not feel proud enough of my production to want thee to hear it. I enclose a programme of the next day, however, and I will let thee come then.

"Our little meetings became so dead and cold, that we thought it best to stop them; and Charlie feeling the need of something in their place, asked me to meet with him just to read a chapter every morning. We began to meet, and pretty soon some one else came; then another, and another, and now there are five of us. It seems as if the Lord must have sent them, for we did not ask them. We have really nice times up there, no formality about it. Sometimes we pray after reading, and sometimes not—just as we feel.

"How we can carry Christ into everything, can't we? Yesterday I was being examined in Geometry, and I found there was one question that I could not answer. So I prayed that it might be shown to me, and then left it, and went on answering the others. When I had finished them, I came back, and studied over that question, and just fifteen minutes before the time for handing in the answers, I found out how to do it. Without help I do not think I could have done it."

On the 3d of July he wrote in his Diary:

"Yesterday, Professor Hartshorne gave us a farewell address, in which he showed forcibly the power and influence for good that one upright moral man might have in a community. Oh! if by my manliness I could have such an influence in my class! I have prayed for help to do exactly as I should here, so as to bring the most glory to God, and I am trusting for an answer. Next year I shall be a Soph, and the temptations to disobey all rules, and do just as I please, will be very great! I shall want to 'rush,' and all that; and yet I know it is not right; so may the Lord give me help to stand up for Him, and not to do anything next year, nor this either, that will dishonor Him at all."

On the 11th he wrote.

"Spouting night! I feel, I feel, I feel, I feel just like a whale! Got through tolerably; M. was delighted with the old thing, which rather discourages me. Subject — 'The fear of Peculiarity.'"

On the 12th, Frank came home for the summer vacation, to the unqualified joy of the whole colony at "The Cedars," and of his especial friends M., W., and B., in particular. Although such a wonderful change had taken place in his Christian experience, since last they had met in this happy summer home, yet dear Frank had not been spoiled by it for the old accustomed days of fun and adventure. With a greater zest than ever, because with a heart at peace with God, he could throw himself into all the innocent pleasures of which these summers at "The Cedars" were so full; and we mothers lived our young lives over again, as we sympathized, and cautioned, and helped in the daily sports and adventures. Very few records are left of this summer vacation, except the bright memories of a light-hearted, happy, manly boy, drinking in to the full the cup of youthful joys.

On the 3d of August Frank went to Newport, where he spent about three weeks, meeting there most of the "Hestonville party," and having a good merry time. From there he wrote to me:

"MY DEAREST MOTHER:

"I ought to have written before, I expect, but it is very hard to write here. I began several letters, but as soon as I would get under good headway, in would come somebody and say, 'Come on, let's take a sail.' So off I would go, and resolutely make up my mind to write when I came back. But then it would be: 'Let's go rowing;' or, 'Let's take a walk;' or, 'We are going to see the girls, won't you come?' or something of that kind. So I have been just on the go all the time. Charlie and I sleep together, and the other two in an opening room, and it is a perfectly jolly crowd. There is something going on all the time with us, either sailing, rowing, walking, or being with the girls. So I am having as elegant a time as is possible, and would not have missed it for anything.

"The order of exercises generally amounts to this. From seven till eight waking up by pillow-fights, and dressing. From eight to nine breakfast, and afterwards reading the Bible, — we four together. From nine to two, either a good long sail, or else waiting on the girls; and in the afternoon and evening ditto. We had a sail yesterday by ourselves to the Lightship, about four miles out in the ocean. It was very rough, and the spray dashed all over us, so we came home soaked. But it was splendid, I tell thee, managing the boat all ourselves, out in an unusually rough sea, and quite a high wind."

One of the Hestonville party, a young lady, who was at Newport at this time, among other reminiscences of dear Frank, writes:

"He conducted our last prayer-meeting at Newport, in the summer of 1871. It was the day he took the sail up to Rocky Point, and he came in tired; but led the meeting, I remember, with great power and earnestness. He chose the last chapter of Revelation, and spoke especially of the seventeenth verse, 'And let him that heareth, say come,' and he brought it out very impressively. How fully he lived up to it in his own daily life! His conversation seemed so much in heaven. In connection with this verse in Revelation, and the subject of inviting others to the Saviour, and confessing Him before men, he quoted Matt. v. 16, very beautifully. He said, 'Let your light shine, — *let*, not *make*. God has given us the light, now we must let it shine.' It was a very solemn meeting, and after it was over, we three sat on our doorstep for a long time, talking, especially of trust, I think, and of the work which lay before all of us; of the many temptations we all had, and the responsibilities which rested upon us as men and women,— the many points of temptation for men, and their opportunities for service, and woman's work in preparing them for it. And as trust was talked of, I remember so well how we all felt, that whatever was before us, we need not fear, but trusting in God, we might be sure it would all be right."

So sweetly and naturally were the innocent pleasures and religious interests of our boy's life intermingled, that each seemed to grow spontaneously out of the other; and while his Christian faith never lessened his enjoyment of all the good things belonging to his youth, but rather strengthened it, neither did participation in these weaken his earnest pursuit after heavenly things, nor dim the sweet sense of his Saviour's love. Eminently natural in his whole Christian experience, he seemed to have lived long enough to taste largely of earth's joys when sanctified by grace, that he might exemplify the wonderful adaptability of the religion of Jesus to our human nature in all its stages, and to show that it was intended to make us happy in every right sense of that word. Then, this mission being fulfilled, our son was to be taken home to eternal happiness in Heaven, just as he had reached an age when the cares and trials of life must almost inevitably have come upon him, and from which our fondest love could not have shielded him; and it has seemed to us sometimes that his Lord permitted a life of such unusual purity and happiness to end thus early, in order that in the company around the Throne his voice may sound a different tone from that of the multitude of those who have "come through great tribulation," to swell the grand chorus of praise.

CHAPTER X.

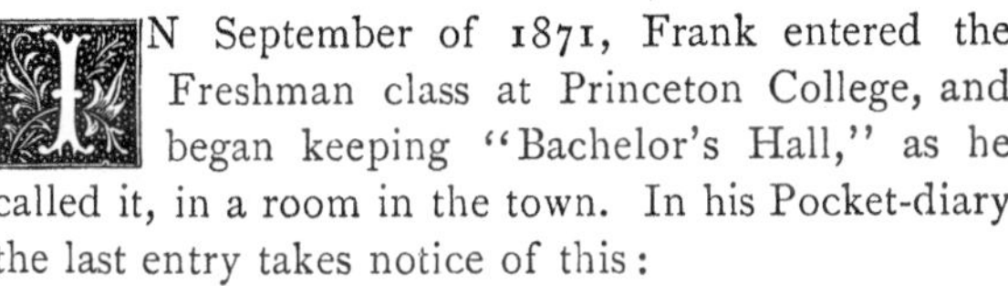

IN September of 1871, Frank entered the Freshman class at Princeton College, and began keeping "Bachelor's Hall," as he called it, in a room in the town. In his Pocket-diary the last entry takes notice of this:

"*September* 13*th*. Oh, thou poor diary, thou dost tell but little of my thoughts and feelings, so lazy am I about writing in thee! And now what am I? Still I do hope a trusting child of God! And where? Well, of all places in the world, in Princeton. Yes, here at college; here, if nothing happens, for four years, for better and for worse. Princeton will still keep me a member of '75, if I live and remain well. Jean Ingelow says, in her 'Songs of Seven,' something like this: 'Ring out, ye bells, ring out your wild changes!' And I thought of this, as I heard the college-bell ring to-night, here at Princeton, in my own private room. How changed is my position from this time last year."

On the same day he wrote to me:

"DARLING MOTHER:

"Here I am, safe and sound, in my Bachelor's Hall at 7½ P. M.; arrived about one.

. . . .

"I don't like to confess it, but I feel really lonely to-night. I would not for the world acknowledge I was homesick; but I should not mind one bit being at 'The Cedars' with thee just now. It is a dreadful shame I do not let out my real feelings when I am at home, but it seems almost impossible. Those talks thee had with me, that prayer of thine by my bedside the night before I left, and all thy loving advice, was ever so acceptable, and more profitable to me than I can tell; and yet I hardly gave thee the slightest sign of sympathy, thereby depriving us both of a great deal of pleasure. It sometimes seems to me as if it must be hard work loving me. I am so cold, and there is so little sign of feeling about me. However, I know thee does love me, and thee cannot tell how much I think about it, when I am not with thee. That coldness is undoubtedly a defect, which I want to try and overcome. My trust is all in the Lord, and was so while I was at home; but I did not talk about it. He will keep me, I am sure.

"Give much love to Mary and the 'young uns,' and an untold amount for the dear mother of

"F. W. S."

To his father, also, he wrote on the same day:

"DARLING FATHER:

"I feel ever so lonely here, not knowing a soul; but I will not acknowledge I am homesick. I shall, nevertheless, be very glad to see thee when thee comes. You never know how much you love people until you are separated from them. I never had the faculty of expressing my love to thee and mother, —

but, indeed, I do love you, and try to observe your wishes a great deal more than perhaps you know; and in coming here, I think I appreciate fully your kindness in giving me a good thorough education, and in keeping me so liberally while doing it. And now that I know, in some degree, the advantages of education, I can never be thankful enough to my Heavenly Father for so loving a father and mother; nor to my earthly father for so many opportunities others, more worthy, are longing for and cannot have. And, father, I do want to put my thanks in a tangible shape, by being a thorough, industrious student, and a good son; but, knowing I cannot accomplish this by my own strength, I have once more afresh given myself wholly into Christ's care, and He, I am sure, will keep me from the many temptations which are acknowledged to beset us here on every side."

On the 17th he wrote to his "Auntie Lill":

"My very dear Auntie:

"Few letters were ever more acceptable to me than thy last. It came the night after I had arrived here; and all day, not knowing a person to speak to, I had been feeling very lonely, and very much shut out from almost everything; and then came thy letter, and I read it and re-read it, and it seemed to be so pleasant to be reminded that the dear people at 'Ivy Lodge' were remembering me. Of course, I knew in a general way that you were thinking of me and praying for me, but thy letter seemed to bring it home with a great deal of force. It was so comforting to know, that, although the people around me did not care for me in the least, yet there was some one who did, and who was kind enough to say so just when I felt so lonely. I am getting acquainted gradually, but thee knows it is a slow process for me.

"One thing I enjoy more in consequence of being such a stranger, and that is communion with Christ. He seems like such an old and tried Friend now. I know He is watching over and guiding me, and so I do not fear but that all will turn out right.

"We have Class prayer-meetings and College prayer-meetings, both of which I expect to attend. As the first one comes to-night, I am praying for help and strength to take whatever part in them it may be the Lord's will I should take; and I am sure He will enable me to do it. It is a great comfort to me to think that thee is praying for me, and I will indeed do as much for thee."

After this meeting, Frank wrote to me:

"The prayer-meeting our class had to-night was very good indeed; almost every one spoke or prayed, although it was the first; there was no holding back nor reluctance. With Christ helping me, I was enabled to pray. One thing I noticed, their prayers were too roundabout and general — not so much for themselves as for every one else."

On the 24th he wrote to me:

"My stove is put up in my room, and a stock of wood laid in, and I have had a fire the last few days. This is really quite cheerful. I love to put out the light, and sit down in front of the open draught, and watch the fire flickering, and then dream about home and you all, and my future prospects, and my present work,—such work as the Lord, I humbly believe, has appointed for me, but for which, alas ! I am all too unworthy. I have often thought that the reason God gives some of His work to the weakest of His children, is to show them their absolute need of Him, — that they can do nothing without His aid. I believe thee was right in saying it was my privilege to preach the 'Higher Christian Life' here. But, oh, I feel so utterly unable to do it in the right way ! And so I have just resigned it all into the Lord's hands. When He wants me to speak for His glory, He will tell me what to say and then I need fear no blunder. It is such a comfort to remember, that, if I am under His guidance, He will not let His cause suffer.

"I am getting gradually acquainted, but have not yet found the fellow I would care to be intimate with. He is here, though, I suppose. This life, where I have to back myself socially, is bringing me out somewhat, I hope. Father told thee, I suppose, about our cane-fight ; how we Freshmen undertook to carry canes, and the Sophs tried to take them away. And how we held on to them, and how I came out victorious, though with a broken cane and scratched hands. Oh, it was jolly fun ! "

On the 1st of October, he wrote :

"The prayer - meeting, last Sunday, was very interesting. I said a little about trusting Christ. But there are so many older Christians there, that I hardly like to say anything that seems like giving advice. My own experience, during the past week, has been very restful, more so than ever before. I am trying, all the while, thy plan of a total surrender. It seems so wonderful to have my every action guided by the Lord, and to be enabled to follow that guidance."

In my reply to this letter, I wrote:

"I rejoice over thy experience, my dear boy. It only remains for thee now to keep thy heart with all diligence. And the way to *keep* it, is to *abandon* it to the care and keeping of thy Lord. I am so thankful thee knows the *rest* of faith. This always comes when there is a childlike confidence in Jesus, which clings to His word, and will not give heed to a doubt. Of course He will save thee, for this is just what He came to do. And when all thy cares are cast on Him, He will keep thy heart and mind in perfect peace. I am very glad thee spoke in the prayer-meeting about it. Thy youth need not hinder thee in the least, because we are told that God has ordained praise out of the mouths of babes. Thee will invariably find that confession will greatly strengthen thy faith. And the clearer and more definite thy confession can be, the better for thy own soul. I find a bold, clear, confession is one of the surest ways of baffling Satan, when he comes with his suggestions of doubt and discouragement."

CHAPTER XI.

ON the 15th, Frank wrote:

"I had a talk yesterday with a fellow here that interested me very much. He began to explain to me the 'dreadful doctrine of full sanctification' held by the Methodists. I asked him why it was so dreadful, and explained it a little; how it was only trusting Christ to keep us moment by moment. And, finally, he said he could not argue against it, only he could not see how man, who is sinful by nature, could possibly help that nature coming out. I told him I would lend him father's book on 'Holiness through Faith,' which might perhaps enlighten him; and he promised to read it.

"My experience is very blessed. No especial feeling, but just a restful sense that Christ is purifying me and taking care of me. I cannot keep my thoughts on Him as much as I should like, but it is getting easier to do so all the time."

On the 20th he wrote to his aunt:

"One good thing I have to report, and that is that I am altogether over my loneliness. There is a very pleasant fellow, who rooms opposite to me, and we spend the evenings talking about politics, etc. He is a Democrat. Then, in the daytime, between playing football and studying, my time goes pretty rapidly, and I was really surprised, the other day, to find that October was nearly three-quarters gone.

"My room looks quite nice now with all the pictures hung up. . . . .

"The Lord is keeping me wonderfully, I feel most truly thankful to say, and does enable me, despite my great diffidence, to speak sometimes for Him."

On the 22d he wrote to me:

"Darling Mother:

"I suppose I could come home next Sixth-day, and I would like to be there while Mr. Inskip is there. How are his meetings? As interesting as ever? I think I need some help; for, although I am trusting to a certain degree, and am kept to that degree wonderfully, yet somehow I lack that full and entire surrender and the looking to Christ for guidance as much as I should. Principally I am weak in the working point; that is, I cannot expect to be kept, unless I often exert myself to work for Christ; and just there I do appear to be failing. I seem to need wisdom as to how to do it best; and I feel too afraid to try to work, for fear I shall not do it in the best way. I 'll acknowledge this is wrong, but somehow I cannot help it; and so I think I need help from above, to enable me to 'ask for wisdom, nothing wavering.'

"There is undoubtedly a great field for work here. In the prayer-meeting last night, when I heard several earnest prayers for a revival, and heard them say they knew the revival must begin in our own hearts, I thought of what a glorious gospel I had to tell them, and yet lacked wisdom to know how to tell it in the best way. Oh, how I would like to tell each one how I am kept, and how sweet and restful my life is! Do, please, pray that I may have this wisdom.

"I had the most beautiful row yesterday that could be. A Junior and I started off, and came to what looked like a mill-pond, on which were some boats; we unlocked one, got two flat sticks for paddles, and went up to what appeared like the head of the pond; there was a narrow stream flowing in at this place, and we followed up its course for about three miles, right into the heart of a dense swamp, with old, romantic oaks and maples bending over on each side, and bushes so thick that we could not see ten feet either way. Altogether it was so perfectly enchanting and romantic, that I was entirely carried away; and, to crown all, we started up a lot of wild ducks. . . . .

"I have found a fellow at last that I believe I like. He is an earnest Christian, and full of fun, ready to go on all sorts of adventures, stronger than I am, and one of those whole-hearted fellows who, whatever he undertakes, will do it well."

Frank came home as proposed, and spent two or three days, attending the meetings for the promotion of Christian Holiness, being held in Philadelphia, at that time, by Mr. Inskip and Mr. McDonald. He was deeply interested, and seemed to find the needed help he spoke of in his last letter. On the 5th of November, he wrote to one of his young friends concerning it:

"Dear D.:

"I was at home last Seventh and First-days, but failed to get a glimpse of thy countenance, as my time was mostly taken up going to the meetings held by Mr. Inskip and Mr. McDonald, in the Fourth Street Church. Did thee get to any of them? They were most certainly splendid meetings, and helped me on my way wonderfully. I shall never forget one, in which Mr. I. asked all who would then and there solemnly consecrate themselves without reserve to God, to raise their right hands. It seemed so solemn, that at first I was almost afraid, but was helped to do it, and have often since been unspeakably thankful for it. After that he asked all who felt willing to trust Christ, then and there, to give them a *pure heart,* to do the same. Again faith triumphed, and again my hand went up. And, indeed, D., although my former experience was very blessed, it did not at all come up to this. As long as I continue trusting, a perfectly cloudless sky is between me and Christ. And if for a moment I look away, immediately it sends a pang through me, as if something had happened to make me unhappy.

"Do, I beg of thee, try it, if thee has not already. It is just simple faith, believing implicitly what Christ says.

"And I am sure if Christ can give me this faith, He also can thee. For here I am among a lot of fellows who are violently opposed to this doctrine, called on to declare it to them, and to tell them I have experienced it. And then I must expect to be watched closely, that they may see whether I live a true doctrine. Surely Christ will give thee this faith too.

"The difference between a pure heart, and one where sin to a certain extent still exists, is something like this, I think. When our hearts are pure, we are, as it were, on the highway of holiness, and that is holy, and the devil cannot come on it to tempt us. He does come alongside, and holds out his allurements, but unless we walk up to him and take these, he cannot touch us. As long as we are in the middle, we are safe. But where the heart is not pure, we are, as it were, travelling on the same road with Satan. And although using Christ's strength to keep him under most of the time, still if we are not very careful, continually looking out for him, he will trip us up somehow or another. Because, in this last case, he has our sinful nature to work on, without any deliberate act on our part, while in the other case it requires this deliberate act of leaving Christ, before we can be overcome.

"That is as plainly as I can put it; but, anyhow, the truth is the same. Christ will cleanse our hearts, if we will trust Him to do it.

"A very good plan, I find, when a temptation is coming, is to say to myself over and over, 'Jesus saves me, Jesus saves me.' And although at first it may seem untrue, still in the end you are sure to be victorious.

"Tell me in thy next letter that thy heart is purified by Christ's blood. Thankful I am beyond expression that mine is.

"But my enjoyment in talking about how much has been done for me is so great, that I have gone beyond my usual limit to my letters, which thee must excuse. I shall pray that the next letter that comes from thee, will tell me of one more who has entered into the 'rest of faith;' and I hope thee also will pray that I may be kept within the truly blessed 'highway of holiness,' and may turn neither to the right nor the left. Thy attached brother in Christ,

"FRANK W. SMITH."

We had urged our dear boy, while with us on this memorable visit, on his return to College to make a good confession among his fellow-students of what the Lord had done for him; reminding him that the Lord had said to us, "Ye are my witnesses;" and that a man, to be a useful witness, must always tell of what he himself, personally and experimentally, knows of the subject. The very night of his return he did as we had suggested, and thus wrote to me concerning it.

"I got up in our class prayer-meeting the night I returned, and spoke about the necessity of entire consecration, and said I was thankful to say that God had helped me to consecrate myself altogether to Him. But this confession did not seem to make any more impression than if I had not made it. I will not, however, be discouraged, but, with God's help, will do whatever work he has for me earnestly, forgetting self and man, and only looking unto Him. Oh, what a grand thing it is to have any work to do for One who has done so much for us!

"Every time we have a meeting, some one gets up and says what we ought to do; that we ought to do this, or we ought to do that; but no one ever says *how* we are to do it. Does it not seem as if God wanted me to show them the way as it has been shown to me? I have faith Christ will help me this very night to testify for Him, and, having done that, will enable me to live the life of faith I have testified about.

"My visit home did me lots of good. The time when Mr. Inskip asked all in the meeting who would solemnly give their all to Christ to raise their hands, often comes back to me. My hand was up; and, having given myself to Him, not an iota can I take back."

In my reply to this letter, I wrote:

"I have a bad headache to-night, and am almost too tired to write. But my boy must have his letter, if it is only a few lines, that he may know how much I love him. I have been thinking, ever since thee went back, what a darling son thee is, and how proud I am of thee; and I have prayed so fervently that thee may be preserved pure and good in the midst of all the evils around thee. It does seem a great risk to send a young fellow like thee out into such an independent life; but I trust thee to thy Saviour, my boy, and I believe He *will* keep thee. Only thee must keep very close to Him, and never let go thy confidence in Him for a moment. I feel deeply thankful that He is helping thee to take a more decided stand, in witnessing for Him in your meetings. It may not seem to have much effect at first, but it cannot fail, I think, to stir them up in the end; and, anyhow, He has called thee to be His witness; and this is too blessed a secret to be kept hidden away in one's own bosom, — is it not? I do so long for every Christian to know about it, and all seem to be so hungry. Do be faithful, my darling boy, in telling the good news of this full salvation in the Lord Jesus, wherever thee has the least opening.

"The Friends' Biennial First-day School Conference is to be held in Ohio the last of this month, and I want thee to go to it very much, for I expect it will be a time of feasting spiritually. Does thee think they will let thee off from College, if I write very urgently? It will take a whole week, as we leave on the 20th, and do not get back until the 28th."

We had always felt that to foster and stimulate our boy's religious life was, after all, the matter of chiefest importance; and whenever there were any especially desirable Christian privileges to be enjoyed, of the kind he would appreciate and like, we never hesitated to let him take a holiday from his studies, in order to avail himself of them. It was arranged, therefore, that he should go on this Western trip with a large party of friends who were going out from Philadelphia.

On the 12th of November he wrote, asking what things he should bring home for the journey, and then continued:

"Last night at the prayer-meeting, in the College, Mr. H., a most earnest Christian, asked all who would be willing to make one personal effort to save some soul, to stand up. I was not there, as I had been out gunning; but M. told me, nearly every one stood up, and that the meeting was very solemn. Oh, how I do pray there may be a revival here! I have prayed for help, and do believe I shall have it, to be in the foremost ranks of any movement to help on the work of Christ. I have been most wofully negligent in this particular, but Christ is waking me up. I have faith that this very night I shall be helped to take a bold stand on Christ's side. I mean, I shall be enabled to say something definite, marking my position. I shall leave this letter open to tell thee about it."

"8 O'CLOCK.

"I was at prayer-meeting, and my backwardness kept me from rising at first, as a good many others rose pretty rapidly; and I was afraid I should have to keep still altogether, until near the end I prayed for one more chance, and then I was called on to close the meeting by prayer. So I prayed God would show us our privileges in Christ, and would fill us with His Spirit; but that is not decided nor plain enough for me, and I shall pray that strength may be given me to come out more boldly on the Lord's side.

"I found this afternoon that there was one thing I had to give up, and that was a regard for my reputation; and grace was given me to do it; and now I feel willing to be accounted anything for Christ; though, of course, I want to be very sure it is for Christ, and nothing else."

To his friend C. H., he wrote on the same date:

". . . . And now, Charlie, about our own personal experience, which we have so often talked over together. I did not half appreciate my privileges at Haverford, where there was a little band of us so fully in sympathy. Here almost every one, even the Christians, are opposed to the doctrine of sanctification by faith; and it is very hard 'clinging to the cross' without any sympathy. But what is a faith worth which cannot hold on to Christ through thick and thin? And because there is so little sympathy, Christ has drawn me more to Himself, and my experience is, I think, richer and richer all the time. Oh, how much Christ has done for you and me! We ought to be so thankful, that we would be willing to do anything for Him. I pray often that you may be built up in the most holy faith, and that you may be enabled to follow Christ's guidance in *all* things!

"I have come lately to a very blessed experience of entire rest in Christ. The life of trust, where one has to have a fight for faith, when each particular sin comes up, is after all only a partial rest. But it is blessed to trust for heart purity, which brings an *abiding* faith, and this I am learning now. I send you some texts on the subject, to show you that this is taught in the Bible. Look the subject up, and if you do not realize it, pray that you may."

In this letter, and in the one to "D.," on the 5th of November, Frank touches upon a subject which is one of the utmost importance to those who seek to enter into the possession of all the privileges that are ours in Christ. As he well expresses it, "to have a fight for faith as each particular sin comes up, is after all but a partial rest;" and yet many who enter into the life of faith do not get further than this. The lesson is learned, that *when* we trust, Christ delivers; but the secret of being *kept* continually trusting is not yet found out. The soul in this condition is like a general, guarding his outposts, and always able to defend them against the assaults of the enemy, when he reaches the spot in time; but who is continually harassed in all his movements by a traitor in his castle at home, whose constant aim it is to betray him into the hands of his enemies. This traitor is inbred sin. And in order to know a complete and continuous victory, this inward enemy must be cast out, and the heart must be cleansed from all unrighteousness. Then, the very centre of the being having been taken possession of by Christ, and all His enemies destroyed by His presence, He reigns there supreme. And the soul finds itself "kept by the power of God," through an unwavering faith, which nothing jostles or dims. This wonderful truth is taught in many ways, and under many different figures, in the New Testament. Being "dead to sin," knowing "the body of sin to be destroyed," "purifying our hearts by faith," being "cleansed from all unrighteousness;" all these, and many other expressions, set forth this truth, that Christ, who was manifested to destroy the works of the devil, is able and willing to destroy his very worst work,—even that which he wrought in us when he implanted sin in our nature. And that when Christ enters there, sin must retire. But let it be understood that it is only the presence of Christ that keeps out the sin. There is no inherent purity in the heart itself. But as with light and darkness, so with Christ and sin; they cannot exist together, there is no possibility of fellowship between them. Let a room, however, presume on its light, and shut out the rays of the sun, and darkness at once fills it. So let the soul presume on its purity, and cease to let Christ abide in it, and that moment sin reigns there again supreme. The indwelling presence of Christ makes the heart pure, and keeps it pure. The indwelling presence of Christ drives out His enemies, and keeps them out. The indwelling presence of Christ destroys (or "renders inert") the body of sin, and keeps it so; but the moment the soul lets go of Christ, or turns its eyes away from Him, that moment its old evil all returns. Thus we see that our great need is to abide in Christ continuously, and all else will be right, for He will take care of it. And our great danger lies in being betrayed out of that abiding, for then all else goes wrong. "Christ formed within" is our sure defence against all our enemies, and our sure deliverance from our inward foe. In learning this blessed secret, our dear Frank realized a deliverance far greater than any he had yet known, and from henceforth his life flowed on in a sweet accord with the will of God, knowing but slight variations from a perfect inward rest.

CHAPTER XII.

ON the 20th of November we started for Wilmington, Ohio, where the First-day School Conference was to be held. We reached there the next day. Some other young Christians, who also knew this blessed 'rest of faith,' were of the party, and Frank greatly enjoyed the sweet fellowship they all had with one another, as they travelled on together.

The Conference was a deeply interesting and stirring time to all who were present, and Frank entered with great earnestness into all the various meetings, and enjoyed exceedingly the discussions on the subjects connected with and growing out of Sunday School work. His principal enjoyment, however, was found in the little side-meetings for the promotion of Christian holiness, which were held between the regular sessions of the Conference. He had so sweetly realized in his own consciousness the blessedness of the rest of faith, that he rejoiced in every means taken to bring his fellow-Christians into the same happy experience; and it was always a very precious help to me, when laboring in these meetings, to look into the happy, peaceful face of my son, and to know that he himself was a living proof of the truths we were trying to teach. He took some little part in these meetings, but felt that his place there was rather that of a learner, to gather strength and wisdom for his work at Princeton, and among his young friends. It was a time of great blessing to him, and he thus wrote to his "Aunty Lill," soon after his return:

"It seems to me that the Conference at Wilmington must have been a wonderful blessing to a great many. I know it was to me. I never had such entire trust before. That beautiful text, 'Thou wilt keep him in perfect peace whose mind is stayed on Thee, because he trusteth in Thee,' has been ringing in my ears ever since my return, and has really been my experience most of the time. Once or twice, I am sorry to say, I have let in some worry, and have destroyed my peace for awhile. But Christ has restored it to me again. Oh what a Saviour He is! It does seem like asking so much to have Him take us with all our frettings, and worryings, and doubts; but He has promised.

"I spoke in our class prayer-meeting last Second-day about this perfect peace, and confessed that I enjoyed it. It did not seem to make much impression, but still I believe it was right for me to do it; and I do pray that the Holy Spirit will give some one a longing for it. I do so want to do some work for Christ who has done so much for me."

The year 1872, destined to be the last of his life, though we little dreamed it then, opened thus peacefully on our precious boy, and from this time forward the text he quoted to his aunt seemed to have become the sweet undertone of his life. To his friend C. H. he also referred to it, in a letter written at this time:

"As to my own religious experience, it has been *wonderful.* This text has been my watchword ever since I came back from the Conference; 'Thou wilt keep him in perfect peace whose mind is stayed on thee, because he trusteth in thee.' I never had such trust, such peace, and such a feeling of the nearness of Christ before. I don't worry about the future, God will take care of it; for the present I am trusting. I often remember you in my prayers, and ask that you may continue to find this blessed, thrice blessed peace and joy."

Having thus found such perfect rest in his own soul, Frank began to feel more than ever anxious to work for others, and he was greatly grieved when he found that for a little while his natural reserve and timidity seemed to stand in his way. His father wrote to him in reference to this as follows:

"My Dear Son:

"I want thee to feel the weight of debtor, that thee owes to the students around thee; for 'we are debtors to all men,' says the Apostle. Let thy light shine; Christ is thy light. Do not cover up or hide the precious things taught thee; the ice once broken, it is the most delightful thing to talk of Jesus and His grace. A habit of unhappy reticence continued in now, may blight all thy future life. The hiding of the talent means something! Thee has learned to trust

Jesus for victories over sin and self; now, in the same way, trust Him to enable thee to speak for Him joyfully and easily. Tell me, if thee can, that faith has conquered thy natural reticence; few things are more longed for now by me. Lovingly,

"THY FATHER."

On his return to College, after the Christmas holidays, Frank wrote to me, on the 14th of January, on this subject:

"DEAREST MOTHER:

"I am all settled now, and am just as comfortable and snug here in my new room as a 'bug in a rug.' And I am very happy. But I am troubled that I do not make more efforts to work for Christ, at the most only a spasmodical one here and there. Why is it that I can't seem able to work? Yesterday, as I was taking a walk, I thought, 'Why can't I on my walks distribute tracts?' But I shrank somewhat from the idea; I thought I was more given up than that. I am willing enough to speak twice a week in my class prayer-meeting, — my reluctance to that I gave up long ago; but when it comes to speaking in private to a few fellows, who I feel sure are not interested, my faith seems to give out, and I can't find words. And the idea of distributing tracts, or of speaking in the College prayer-meeting, seems equally hard. And I do not know what to do. What shall I? Pray? I do pray. Trust? I thought I did; but when the time for work comes, I am found wanting.

"It seems almost wrong for me to say I am living

the higher Christian life, until I can record some efforts to further Christ's cause. That the Lord does keep me wonderfully from sins of commission, I know, and I feel most thankful for it; but my faith does not seem to get the victory over my weakness in Christian work; and this is this week's confession."

In my reply I said:

"As to thy work for the Lord, I wish thee could get into that happy place about it, where thee would find it thy greatest joy. I think if once thee could just give all up, and dash into things, and come out boldly as a Christian, so that Christian work would be *expected* of thee, thee would find great liberty in it. I do not believe thee can be happy in any other way. The Lord has done too much for thee, and thy light is too great for thee to keep it always under a bushel. Commit thy ways in this unto the Lord, dear boy, and He will direct thy steps. Ask Him to *make* thee willing to work, for He can, and He only. But do not stop claiming full salvation, because of this weakness in service; that would be a fatal way of remedying it. Claim it by faith more boldly than ever, for only in this very salvation can thee find any deliverance from thy weakness.

"One thing more. Do not be troubled by any indefinite charges of unfaithfulness, as though thee ought to have done a great deal, but yet thee does not know what. Only be troubled when thee can recall some definite act, when the Lord called and thee refused to obey. Satan makes a great gain when he succeeds in discouraging us with these vast indefinite charges. The Holy Spirit is always definite, and condemns only for definite disobediences or failures. And if nothing has been suggested to thee to do during the day, don't be distressed at night, because thee has done nothing. If God wants thee to do anything, He will tell thee so."

In Frank's next letter, he wrote:

"I don't feel any doubt but that if I should do as thee says, come out so boldly on the Lord's side that Christian work would be expected of me, I should be much happier; but it does seem as if I could not. When I am praying, it seems as if I could do anything, because then I am definitely trusting. But, somehow, when I go out I get interested in studying or exercising, and it seems to become indefinite. Once in a while I am enabled to say a word for Christ, but it seems to have no effect, and this discourages me. Perhaps I ought not to look for fruits, but just trust to the Holy Spirit to guide me, and do as He directs. I will try this, and never mind if my labor does seem fruitless, but just go ahead.

"I am glad thee spoke about those indefinite charges. I have been troubling myself a great deal about them; but now I will not be troubled until some definite act comes before me. To-night, in our College prayer-meeting, I felt that I ought to pray, and I was helped to do it, although it did come rather hard, and I could not have done it without help. So I believe I will give it all into Christ's hands, and I can then trust it will be all right."

About the same time, he wrote to his aunt:

"DEAR AUNTIE:

". . . I am very nicely fixed in my new room in College. The pictures are hung around to suit my taste, and quite set off the white-washed walls. And here I live all alone, 'monarch of all I survey,' with a bright fire, three easy-chairs, a great big sofa, plenty of closet-room, and everything nice and cosy. I would not want to be more comfortable. What kind of plants would be suitable to have in my room?

". . . I have been very much troubled lately about my not doing any work for Christ; and as of course it is a fault in myself, I have tried to remedy it by consecrating myself more fully than ever to the Lord. And I feel sure He will guide me into the right position about it, and will enable me to trust Him to show me when, and where, and how He wants me to speak for Him. Oh, it is such a wonderful relief to be able to cast all my burdens on Him!"

On the 28th of January, he wrote again to his aunt in reference to her little Sabbath-school, in which he always took the deepest interest:

"I do not see how thee can say, aunty, that thee is at all discouraged about thy school, for it has been so wonderfully blessed ever since thee has had it. There have been so many conversions, and the children have all been so much interested. I have always felt sure thee must have a great deal of power with thee there. I pray that thee may, very frequently.

"I do often pray that I too may be able to work acceptably, but sometimes I feel afraid I may have a selfish motive in it. Still I am sure the Lord can manage this.

"I find it harder to keep trusting, and to keep putting my whole dependence upon Christ in prosperity, than in adversity; that is, it is harder when some one tells me of the good influence I have had over him, than when my faults are shown up to me. It is a great lesson to learn that we are most apt to fall when we feel most secure. I am very sorry to hear that about poor ——. He must be leading a wretched life, half trusting and half doubting. I don't think there can be any life more wretched."

To me, he wrote on the same date:

"We had a splendid time on Sixth-day evening. About five o'clock, four of us started to skate on the Delaware to Trenton, about ten miles. The ice was superb; it was full-moon, and altogether just jolly. The only drawback was that one fellow gave out about three miles from Trenton, and we had to pull him the rest of the way. For about one mile I pulled him alone, as the rest gave out also. We reached Trenton a little before nine, got our supper, and lodged at an hotel, as all, except myself, were too tired to skate back that night. Next morning we skated back, and reached Princeton in time for breakfast and chapel. Every one was worn out excepting me; so I, with a party of stronger fellows, started at two on Seventh-day, and went down again, this time in an hour and eighteen minutes, and came back on the cars for supper. Altogether, it was just splendid fun."

From this it will be again seen that Frank's earnest interest in religious subjects, and his deep Christian experience, did not abate in the least his enjoyment of all the sports belonging to his age, nor weaken his energy in heartily carrying them out. And his well-developed manly form, and healthy color, bore witness to the good effects of his fondness for outdoor pursuits. Even when he was taken sick, it seemed almost impossible to believe that so much young life and energy could so suddenly be laid low. And to the very last, death looked as if it must be at least a great way off, even though we were forced to believe it was surely approaching.

In this same letter, quoted above, Frank spoke of his eyes being very weak, and of the idle evenings he was obliged to spend, in consequence of not being able to read or study, and he asked us if he could not hire an organ, that he might amuse himself learning to play and sing. We consented gladly, thankful for an opportunity of gratifying our noble good boy.

On the 4th of February, he went to Trenton to try and hire one, at the same time visiting the family of a dear cousin who resided there. But he found it impossible to accomplish his object, and his father, consequently, bought an organ and sent it up to him, to his great delight.

On the 11th of February, he wrote:

"DEAREST FATHER AND MOTHER:

"I am *perfectly delighted* with my organ. It is such a sweet-toned one, and so handsome. I don't think I ever had anything I enjoyed a quarter as much. There were seventeen fellows up to see it last night, and every one agreed it was a very fine one. Six of the best singers in the College were up here singing and playing, and, I can assure you, there was some delightful music. Surely I can say my cup is running over. I am blessed in almost every way imaginable, especially in having such kind, loving parents. I truly ought to be good.

"I had an elegant time at Trenton, at Cousin B——'s, last week. In the evening we had a very strengthening talk, and I came back here with a much stronger faith. And on Second-day evening I was helped to come out pretty boldly in our prayer-meeting; I spoke on the text in John xvii., 'I pray not that thou shouldst take them out of the world, but that thou shouldst keep them from the evil;' and said I knew for myself that God would answer that prayer, just so far as we had faith to trust Him. After the meeting a fellow came up to my room, and we sat and talked a good while about our experiences. He had not the assurance of faith, and I tried to show it to him, and I think he entered into it."

In Frank's next letter, he touches upon a difficulty very common to young Christians, who feel that unless they are consciously thinking about the Lord all the time, they are doing wrong, and are wandering away from Him; forgetting that the mind cannot be occupied with more than one thing at a time, and that when engaged in studying or playing, it cannot be that we should also be thinking directly on religious subjects.

Frank wrote:

"I have come to the conclusion that my character is not worth much; as soon as I get away from a warming influence, I immediately get cold. I should like to be a bold, strong Christian, but it seems as if, when I stop praying or reading the Bible, I forget about Christ, and become so much interested in what I am doing — studying, reading, or playing — that I do not think of anything religious again all the while. I do not think I do anything wrong particularly; the Lord keeps me to a very great degree from this; but still I do not seem to be an earnest Christian."

In my reply I told Frank, that he was demanding too much from himself; that he could not expect to be always consciously thinking of Christ, when he was busy about other things; that a husband does not cease to love his wife, nor does he care any less to please her when he is busy about his daily occupation, although for hours together perhaps he may scarcely have a thought or remembrance of her; and I urged him to commit himself in this to the Lord, trusting Him to govern his thoughts, and to bring to his remembrance such things as it was His will he should recollect.

To his darling little sister he wrote, on the same day:

"My precious Sister Mary:

"So thee is eight years old, is thee? I am only a little more than twice as old. Hurry up, and maybe thee will catch up to me. Think thee could? I am very much obliged to thee for thy two letters, and I expect thee thinks I ought to have answered them before. Well, so I ought; but I will do it now instead.

"How many Valentines did thee get? I know where one came from. Can thee guess?

"Yesterday two boys came into my room here, and we took off our coats, and pulled the mattress down on to the floor and then turned somersaults on it, like this picture I send thee. Would not thee like to have seen us?

"Do write again to thy loving 'bubba,'

"Frank."

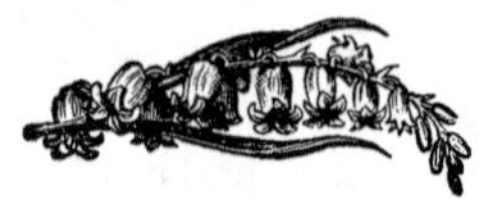

CHAPTER XIII.

ON the 18th of February, Frank wrote home: "There is a little hope at last for our class. I was talking this afternoon with an earnest Christian, and found he just felt the need of this life; so I lent him father's book on 'Holiness through Faith,' and thy 'Word to the Wavering Ones,' and he seemed very glad to get them. He is really in earnest, so now we have agreed to have a little private prayer-meeting every First-day afternoon up in my room. We can only think of six fellows who are enough in earnest to join in it; but, oh, we do want so to be thoroughly stirred up. Do pray for our little private prayer-meeting, that it may tend to bind the few who come more together, and that it may be the means of great blessing to us all. Now please, do not tell this all around; principally, because every one everywhere always comes and praises *me*, whenever they hear of anything of the kind, and I dislike this intensely.

"This fellow I spoke of seemed delighted at the idea of having father to come here and talk to us, and thinks we could get several to come up, especially if they knew long enough beforehand to prepare their lessons."

On the 25th, he wrote to his father:

"DEAREST FATHER:

". . . I heard mother's Bible lesson while I was at home last week, and was deeply interested. I want to begin a deeper study of the Bible for myself; because a truth coming to me directly from the Bible would be so much more vivid than if I had to read it out of some theological work.

"We had our little meeting this afternoon, and a truly sweet time it was. Every one felt the need of a closer walk, and of more earnestness among us Christians; and so, according to thy suggestion, I proposed that we make our next meeting a time for especially looking into the Bible, and seeing if the life thee told us about when thee was here, is possible, and, if so, to enter into it. Do write and tell me a forcible way to present it. I want all the Christians, in our little band at least, to be made perfectly right, and then we can begin to do outside work. We have appointed seven o'clock every morning to pray for each other by name, and for some one erring Christian whom we may pick out. If we are only strong in the Lord ourselves, we can help other weaker Christians so much better. We thought it best for the present to have only those up here to our little meeting, who we are sure are in earnest, and seeking after the right way. As we get stronger, we will invite others in. What does thee think?

"I am so glad we have some definite way of working now. For instance, we agreed that we would all endeavor not to let our class prayer-meetings flag in interest. And we agreed to help each other on once in a while by a comforting word."

In reply to this letter, Frank's father wrote:

"BOSTON, February 27th, 1872.

"MY DEARLY LOVED SON:

"Thy letter is most welcome. I see the hand of God in your being drawn together to seek His full salvation,—I see it in the meeting for self-consecration, which He will wonderfully bless. I look with prayerful hope to a circle, (small at first,) entering into an experience of the joy and power of soul-union with Christ; I see how when *you* are thus right before Him, He can open the very windows of Heaven upon you, and *then* draw in many to share your blessings; and that from the running over of your cup, many shall be led to taste of the water of life, and be saved. I see it all in vision as it were, and feel deeply the importance of your whole-hearted consecration, and accompanying faith. God *could* work without instruments, but he rarely does so; He makes *us* responsible in a most important degree. You may so reflect Christ in the college *through your faith* as to leave His impress upon thousands directly and indirectly. God grant it! is my cry to Him. I have studied the Bible by *subjects*,—with the Concordance almost my only commentary. Take 'pure,' for instance—Can *I* be pure; may *I* 'call on God out of a pure heart,' etc. Or take 'victory,'—or 'dead to sin,'—or 'holy,'—or 'sanctification'; and study them *prayerfully*, earnestly to ascertain what our Lord proposes to do for us. Use the Englishman's Greek Conc ›rdance in preference to the English Concordance.

"Oh my son, how thy father's heart is filled with thanksgiving — (I have been praising God aloud, as I passed along the Boston streets to-day) — that his boy is seeking to walk with God! 'I have no greater joy than to see my children walking in the truth,' as St. John says.

"Thy loving, praying father,

"ROBT. PEARSALL SMITH."

In reference to the work in the class prayer-meetings, which Frank referred to in this letter to his father, we have received since his death a testimony from his room-mate, a member of the Junior class, which shows us how faithfully our dear boy carried out the resolution here expressed.

He writes: "Frank was very highly esteemed by his class, and was a favorite with all, especially the Christians. I have been told that he was the life of the class prayer-meeting, the burden of which chiefly fell on him: and that whenever there was a pause or apparent lack of interest, he was the one to sustain the meeting."

To his friend, C. H., he wrote about this time:

"We have just started a meeting in my room here, something like the one we had at Haverford last year. There are about seven of us, all in earnest to do some work for Christ; and we have just got together to find how best to do it. How is your little meeting coming on? I pray for you all. Oh, Charlie! if you and I can only do some work for Christ! We had such a good start together at Haverford; do let us keep on together. I do so want to be a good, strong, earnest, firm Christian, resting only on Christ, and not at all on myself."

To me he wrote, after their first little meeting:

"DEAREST MOTHER:

"We have had our meeting, and it was really a very sweet time. All who came were very much in earnest. Various plans were set on foot, as how to work for the unconverted, and to help erring Christians; but we all agreed that we had better get right ourselves first. We are going to make 'Holiness' the subject of our next meeting, and inquire and see from Scripture, whether there is such a thing as a close walk with God; and, if so, how to attain it. I do long for us to be completely given up to the service of Christ.

"The fellow I walk with is going to study the Bible with me, and I also want to do it alone. Can thee give me some hints as to how best to study it, the way thee did? It seems to me a great deal of one's power would lie in having studied the Bible for one's self, and not having been satisfied with some other person's thoughts. I want to give at least half an hour a day to this, and I think it will do me more good than simply reading without study; and I have an especial desire too, that P. should be clear and fresh in his knowledge of the truth, as he is going to be a minister. I am sure, it is much better for us to get the truths out for ourselves, than to have to take the opinions of theologians."

In my reply to this letter, I wrote:

"As to studying the Bible, the very best plan is to have a blank-book, ruled in columns, with headings of all the different subjects you are interested in; and then, whenever you come across a text that refers to any one of these subjects, note it down under its respective head. In this way you get subjects thoroughly looked up, and, moreover, have the texts all ready for use. Sometimes, if you want to look up a subject all at once, you can take the 'Concordance,' and take some words that are keys to the subjects, and look at all the texts containing these words. The marginal references also are a great help. It is to my Text-book, arranged on this plan, that I owe most of my knowledge of Scripture. I will send thee a sample-page.

"HOLINESS.

Prayers for Holiness.	*Commands to be Holy.*	*HOW to be Holy.*
Heb. xiii. 20, 21. Phil. i. 9–11. Col. i. 9–14. Eph. i. 15–20. 1 Thess. v. 23, 24. Col. iv. 12. Eph. iii. 14–21. 2 Thess. i. 11, 12. 1 Thess. iii. 9–13. 1 Pet. v. 10, 11.	Rom. xii. 1, 2. 2 Cor. vii. 1. 1 Pet. i. 13–16. Eph. iv. 1–3. Phil. ii. 14, 15. 2 Cor. vi. 14–18. 1 Thess. iv. 1–4, 7. Heb. xii. 14, 15. 1 Pet. ii. 21, 22. Rom. vi. 11–14. Col. iii. 1–5. Eph. iv. 17, 22–24. Eph. v. 1–4. Rom. vi. 1–4. 1 Tim. vi. 11–14. 2 Pet. iii. 14.	Phil. ii. 13. Ps. xliv. 3. Rom. viii. 2–4. Phil. iv. 13. John xv. 4–7. 1 John iii. 6. Gal. ii. 19–21. Gal. v. 24. Rom. xiii. 14. 1 John v. 4, 5. 2 Cor. x. 3–5. Gal. iii. 1–5. Gal. v. 5, 6. Phil. iii. 8–10. Rom. x. 3, 4. Ps. cxliv. 1, 2.

"Any one who will study the Bible in this way cannot fail to become deeply interested in it; and will find that they learn many wondrous things out of God's law."

On the 3d of March, Frank replied:

"DEAREST MOTHER:

"Thy letter was very acceptable, thee may be sure, and I commend thy promptness. I have tried thy plan of studying the Bible, and I find it very interesting. I hope to keep it up regularly.

"We had our meeting again this morning, and it is doing a great deal for us, I hope. I tried to press the necessity of not putting off the entering into this experience of the higher Christian life, but most people seem to look upon it as something to be obtained in the dim and distant future.

"It was ever so nice to see father last night, and I am sure his talk did some good. Several of the fellows have spoken to me about it, and how much interested they were. It stirred them up considerably. What a wonderful help Christian sympathy is. I find it far easier to trust in Christ now, since we have started our meeting, than I did before. I want to take each one of our company and try to impress him individually with the necessity of a consistent walk. Do pray that I may be helped, and that they may be made to feel it necessary. Oh! I do wish we could all get thoroughly melted together in a bond of Christian love!"

Frank's intellectual life was growing rapidly, along

with his spiritual, during this last winter, and he says, writing to us, about this time:

"Princeton has been, and is now, a wonderful thing for me. I am getting more and more earnest every day to improve my mind. I have found another student who feels just as I do about it, and we are reading together daily. He is a Christian, a jolly fellow, smart, has good common sense, and altogether is the nicest companion I have met here yet."

But most of his intellectual interests and aspirations were confided to his Cousin M——, who heartily sympathized with him in them all, and greatly helped him by her advice and encouragement. Some extracts from his letters to her will show how his heart was alive with all noble ambitions, and how he yearned to plunge into life's earnest conflicts. One of his earliest aspirations had been to be a lawyer, and he had often discussed it with her. Writing to her, March 7th, he said:

"And now about that lawyer business. It is hardly worth while to look at it in its poetical light; that it would be a splendid thing to benefit the human race; that I would have a grand chance to bring about reforms; that I could have the love and gratitude of the whole nation; that it would be a worthy cause to strive after, and all that. Just leave this and look at the practical side. *Can* I do it? I am convinced that it is only eloquence that will bring a man favorably before the country, and I know I have not eloquence. I know it by my poor powers of conversation and of writing. And thee knows it too, if thee would only look at the fact in its bare truth. I do not want or need any compliments. I know just what I am worth, and no man or woman alive can make me believe I am eloquent. Thee may say I am not old enough to be developed yet. Granted. I can judge, though, of my comparative abilities by those around me, of my own age, can't I? Hard work, and I don't grudge it, may win me good solid sense, may develop pluck and perseverance, may give me power to express myself plainly, but it can never sharpen my wits, nor give me eloquence.

"Oh, M——, if by sixty years of hard labor I could in one month do anything that would really and truly benefit the world, or even raise the people of our own country so as to help them in eternity, as well as while on earth, I would willingly, more than willingly, do it; for I think I could do true Christian work better in that way than any other. But for this I must have eloquence.

"If, however, I am not a lawyer, my life need not be entirely selfish. If my consecration amounts to anything, it will not be; and if what I do, the world does not stamp as noble and heroic, but passes over in silence, I shall be rewarded in eternity, where eloquence and talent are not necessary."

On the 10th of March he wrote to me:

"We have just had our private prayer-meeting, and it was very interesting. We took the subject of charity, and endeavored to make it practical by promising to try not to say anything evil of any one, and to correct each other, if we heard one another doing it. I suppose we might go on and hunt out an almost innumerable number of Christian virtues, and then, after all, be unable to practise one of them without help from Christ.

"I wish I did not feel so lukewarm between Sundays. I feel all right after writing to thee, and after having our little meeting; but when I begin to enter into the week, reading, studying, or talking about every-day affairs, I feel cold again. I enjoy reading the Bible, I enjoy praying, but still I have that old longing to be nearer Christ, *all* the time near Him, not only on Sundays and in meetings, but when I am busy about everything that I have to do."

Here again Frank made the very common mistake of looking to his feelings, and judging of his spiritual condition by them, instead of by his faith. In my reply I told him this, and urged him to remember that his nearness to Christ did not depend upon his *feeling* near, but upon his trusting; and that, when he was busy at other things and could not be thinking of Christ, he must believe that he was still just as near as in his most fervent moments. I tried to show him that the way of faith, and not the way of feeling, was the safe and happy way; and his heart was comforted, so that he never again expressed a similar trouble.

On the 17th of March he wrote:

"We had a lovely meeting this morning. We took 'Our Father which art in Heaven,' and spoke of the tenderness God displayed by calling Himself Our Father. Then an earnest Christian spoke of the love we should feel towards each other as brethren; and the meeting gradually turned to a practical view of the subject, and we agreed to show more love to each other through the week, and to help and strengthen one another by some little word; also, to endeavor really to do some work in the College. We have become really in earnest, I hope; and agreèd to pray often for a revival, in our own class especially. Oh, I do hope we can do some effective work! It does seem too bad that a band of ten earnest Christians should only speak once or twice a week about the things that interest them most. I do hope we shall do better now, as we have promised each other to do. I know thee is praying for us, and I have faith that thy prayers, and all our prayers, will be answered. If we could only once be thoroughly baptized with the Holy Ghost!

"I was at Trenton, Second-day evening, and received a wonderful lift. We had a lovely meeting, like the H. V. P. used to have last winter, and it did seem so natural and pleasant. It did me a wonderful amount of good."

In reference to these visits to Trenton, of which Frank writes now and then, one of his cousins there has written since his death:

"We have been holding a little prayer-meeting once a week for about two years; and when we heard of Frank's going to Princeton, we thought how pleasant it would be if he could regularly attend them. But owing to some College regulations, he could only be with us occasionally. It was our usual custom to begin our meeting with reading a chapter in the Bible, and then talking about it; and when Frank was with us, we always handed the Bible to him. He used to take it very willingly, but with true humility, which we all noticed to be a marked trait in his Christian character. I remember well his reading a chapter in 1 John. We were all impressed by the solemn and *realizing* way in which he read it; and after he had finished, he spoke of the love of Christ and of holiness very impressively. Our conversation turned naturally to the subject of consecration, and Frank said, that as far as he knew, he was *entirely* the Lord's.

"He used to tell us how he longed to have his life in the College to be such as would show to his fellow-students the truth of what he had openly professed among them,—that he was trusting Jesus to keep him from all sin.

"I wish I could remember more particulars of the deeply interesting occasions when Frank was with us, and of the talks we used to have about the 'life hid with Christ in God,' but I cannot. Frank was always a great help and strength to us."

Another member of this little prayer-meeting also writes:

"At one of our meetings Frank read the chapter ending with the words, 'Be ye therefore perfect, as your Father which is in Heaven is perfect,' and we all were struck with his beautiful and simple explanation of it. He said the little bud was as perfect for a bud, as a full blown rose was a perfect rose; and so we were to be perfect as men, as our Heavenly Father was perfect as God; that we were to be complete in Christ at each stage of our growth, but capable always of a greater maturity of perfection. He always seemed to have so much power to explain things in a clear, simple light. And when we were discouraged, or cast down, he always had some little experience of his own to tell, to help us. And he would try so sweetly to tell us of the love and forbearance of Jesus, that new light would always come into our minds, and a new purpose and resolution into our hearts.

"His prayers were very childlike and full of confidence, just like a little one coming to its Father; and I remember how impressed I was once, when he thanked God with so much simplicity, that we were permitted to come as little children, and call Him 'our Father.' He always brought a power and blessing with him.

"In the first conversation we had with him, after he went to Princeton, he spoke of feeling it his duty to come out decidedly and confess his entire trust in the Lord Jesus; but said he was so anxious to live a right life, and was so sensible of his temptations and his weaknesses, that he had been almost afraid to make such a confession, surrounded as he was by so many who would watch every word and action, and would rejoice in any failure. He asked us to pray in our little meeting that he might have strength to do his duty, and that he might find some who would sympathize and work with him.

"The next time he was with us, he said, in his humble, self-forgetting way, that strength had been given him to acknowledge his Saviour openly and boldly; and that God had sent him one friend who was anxious, like himself, to work for Christ.

"There was one trait in Frank's Christian character that was very rare and beautiful. He never seemed to *think* of such a thing as giving up or being discouraged, but seemed to be always pressing forward."

CHAPTER XIV.

N the 29th of March, Frank's father went to Princeton to spend the Sabbath, and hold meetings with the young men in the Presbyterian Church, with which denomination he was connected.

Frank, being naturally of a very cautious disposition, felt considerable anxiety beforehand, and was proportionably rejoiced when he found how deeply interested all the young men were in the meetings. He wrote to me concerning them from Princeton:

"DEAREST MOTHER:

"Father has had a wonderful series of meetings. There were about two hundred to hear him last night, disagreeable as the weather was; and at the meeting before breakfast, where I hardly expected to see any, there were about thirty; and, at half-past nine, where I told him there might be perhaps fifteen, there were sixty or seventy. The fellows appear deeply interested. Every one seems stirred up, and hopeful of a real revival.

"I had a lovely time at Trenton on Second-day. I think I will try to go down there oftener; it does me so much good."

To his friend C. H. he also wrote, speaking of these meetings and the blessing they had been to himself:

"DEAREST CHARLIE:

"This was delayed, as father was here all day yesterday, having meetings. We really had a wonderful time. Father roused them all on the subject of holiness, and the fellows were deeply interested. I never heard it so plainly stated.—First, a heart purified from all things contrary to the will of God, by the cleansing blood of Christ; and, second, simple and momentary faith in His promises to keep and deliver. I do hope and pray it may result in many entering into this blessed, blessed life.

"I have often thought of what you spoke of as being a good test question,—'Would Christ do this?' and it has been very practical in showing me my duty.

"In letting myself be searched by God's light, I have found many of my opinions have had to be changed. There is one thing, which please don't mention,—it is in reference to becoming a minister. Yes, dear C., after a severe struggle of my will last night, I was helped to say, 'Here am I, Lord, send me in any way Thou pleasest!' It will be a great trial to my flesh, and will go against all my plans for life, and all my prejudices; but if He calls me, He will give me strength to do His will.

"I pray often for you, and for your Bible class. Sanctification is what every band of Christians need. Sinners will not read the Bible; but they will read our lives."

To his beloved "Aunty Lill" he also wrote, concerning these meetings, on the 1st of April:

"My Beloved Aunty:

"Don't think, because I write to-day, that I want to 'April-fool' thee. I did not write before because I really had not time. Father has been here and had some meetings, and they were all very well attended. He spoke very plainly and practically on holiness, and I think they all thoroughly understood what he meant. Two of the fellows said afterwards that it was an experience they themselves had, but in which they had never before found any one to sympathize with them; another came up to me to-day, and said that what he had heard yesterday he had been enabled to put into practical use to-day: 'And it does work,' he said. Oh, I do so hope the result may be real, practical, and widespread through the whole College. All the tracts and books I have to give are in demand. Do pray that we may have a revival here."

During the next week Frank's father stopped at Princeton again, on his way home from Boston, and on the 7th of April Frank wrote:

"Father's meeting this afternoon made a wonderful impression on all who were there. Two or three have told me it was the most solemn meeting they ever attended. One of the most able fellows here said it was the crisis of his life.

"Our own little private prayer-meeting on Sabbath morning was on the words 'Thy will be done;' and after five or six had said how necessary consecration was, not only advisable but necessary, it seemed as if I ought to confess openly to my consecration. This I did, and then said it would be a wonderful comfort to me to hear how the others felt on the subject. It seemed to shut them right up, and only one spoke afterwards on consecration, and he only to confess that he was afraid he was not as fully consecrated as he ought to be. It is a little curious, though natural I suppose, that every one is willing to tell his neighbor, *he* ought to be consecrated, while he himself is not willing to do it."

On the 17th of April the "S. S. S." had a meeting at Baltimore, their last on earth, and they passed a very happy, joyous week together. After Frank's return, he wrote to his cousin M—— concerning it:

"I did have an elegant time in vacation, and at Baltimore. It never was so hard to come back to study. It seemed like coming from one of those wonderful places the opium-eaters describe, back to this dull practical world. I thought, as I came back in the cars, that it was good for us we did not have this much pleasure often, or we would grow blâsé. In fact, I hardly think we could have more fun than we do on some of our S. S. S. parties.

"I have been wondering, since I came back, whether it is the best thing in the world for me to have my mind filled with an indescribable, romantic, day-dreamish sort of a desire to do, and to be, something great. I mean, whether I had not better leave the romantic side of life, and deal simply with the practical. It is all very well to have high and noble resolves, and to be able to think of them as really noble. But after all, who accomplish the most,—the dreamers, or those who quietly let go all ideas of doing anything grand, and simply throw themselves into the practical work around them?

"Whenever I get too enthusiastic over my future prospects, I always throw a damper on myself by remembering that every one who is young and strong, and in good health, starts in life with a wonderful determination to do everything. But when he comes to fight the battle, he finds that he fails. Now, why should thee, or B., or I, be any more likely to succeed than the thousands of others who have been just as ambitious and just as talented?

"But vale, vale! Sadly, because the S. S. S. is over, perhaps the last; joyfully, because life and next summer are ahead!"

On his return to Princeton at this time, Frank joined with a Junior in taking some very pleasant rooms, consisting of a common parlor, with a private bed-room for each, opening into it. And he greatly enjoyed the change in many ways. The Christian fellowship of his room-mate was very delightful to him, and they seemed to be a mutual help and strength to each other. This room-mate, in writing to us, since our boy's death, says:

"He was a most genial, pleasant room-mate, and we had a great deal of enjoyment, in the short time we were together. I have often said that I did not think I could have found a pleasanter companion.

"We were in the habit of having 'family worship'

together in our parlor every night before we retired to our own rooms, and were thus wonderfully drawn together in our religious life. One evening I would read a passage in the Bible, and he would lead in prayer, and the next he would read, and I would pray. We were reading through Acts. We often had long talks on our religious views, which I enjoyed very much. And although we might not agree exactly, yet we always separated with a greater respect for each other's opinions, and there were very few points on which we differed."

On the 28th, he wrote to his little sister Mary:

"DEAR LITTLE SISTER:

"It is ever so good in thee to write to me. Maybe, when thee goes to College, and I get little again, I will write to thee. How are thy poor measles? Has thee let them go away yet? I should think they would get tired of staying with thee so long.

"Did n't thee tell me one morning, when we were having a frolic together, that thee sometimes sees ghosts? Well, I went down to the graveyard last night, all in the dark, to look for a ghost, and what does thee think I saw? Nothing at all but a few grave-stones! I guess there are no ghosts, and thee only *thinks* thee sees something.

"I am so glad, my precious sister, that papa is able to tell me thee is a real Christian, trying to be good. It makes me love thee more and more. Write a letter to thy bubba, who loves thee ever so much.

"FRANK."

On the same day, he wrote to me:

"DEAREST MOTHER:

"All safe back here, and delightfully fixed in my new quarters. But it has seemed harder to come back this session than it ever has before. I don't know why it should; but in order to conquer it, I have plunged deeply into work. I am not homesick; but guess I had too good a time in vacation with the 'S. S. S.,' etc.

"I forgot to bring any books or tracts of yours on Holiness back with me, and two or three have asked for them. Thee had better send me a small package by express. One fellow told me he wrote to his mother about this Higher Life, not knowing but she would disapprove of it. She wrote back a long letter, saying it was just what she had believed for a long while, but that she had never seen any book on it except Boardman's. He wants some of ours to send to her. I think there are several here who have entered into the experience, but who do not seem to want to tell it. I expect thee would say I am one. Perhaps I am, but I have told it once or twice, and met with but little response, and it seems to have shut me up. Not right, I suppose.

"Don't thee think a cultivated intellectual life is likely to kill the spiritual? How are you to reconcile the two? Drop the intellectual? I do not mean, of course, to say that my intellect is very cultivated, but I can see that when I get particularly zealous to improve it, I seem to grow lukewarm spiritually. Now it seems to be right and necessary for me, here at College at least, to cultivate my mind; and yet I do not want to kill my spiritual life in doing it. Do tell me where the medium is to be found. It is a question I have been puzzling over for a good while.

"Thee cannot imagine how intense a desire has been slowly begetting itself in me for a long time to cultivate my mind, and I must now settle the question. If I should have to give up all means of mental improvement, and become an uneducated preacher for instance, thee cannot tell what a trial it would be to me. This is a sticking-point with me, I think, though I never defined it before.

"It does seem to me sometimes that my lot in life is almost too happy to be true. I have so many things to be thankful for. Just suppose I could never write in this way to thee or father, like some boys I know, who never write more than two pages home, simply because they get no sympathy. If the older we grow the more enjoyment we have, I do not know where I will end, I am so happy now."

On May 1st I replied to Frank's question in this letter, as follows:

"As to thy question about intellectual cultivation, that is thy present duty; therefore it need not, and ought not, to hinder thy spiritual life. I do not think there is anything in intellectual pursuits that is necessarily deadening, any more than there is in any other pursuit. Religion is made to *fit into* our human life here, with all its needs and all its capabilities; and it only needs for us, whatever we do, even if it be eating and drinking, to do it to the glory of God, and all will adjust itself in harmony with His will. I believe it is the duty of every one to obtain the best education possible; and if thee only looks at thy studies as being thy duty, and as being really pleasing to God, and then asks His blessing continually on thy efforts, I think thee will not find them deadening. It is a great disadvantage to a preacher to be uneducated; but, if he finds himself so, he must do the best he can with it. If, however, he has an opportunity to remedy it, it is his bounden duty to do so. Commit this matter to the Lord, dear boy, and trust Him to keep thee fresh and bright in thy spiritual life, and it will all be right."

In Frank's reply to this letter, he wrote:

"I did not mean exactly that kind of intellectual cultivation thee referred too; of course, it is my duty to get the best education I can, while you are keeping me here; but what I meant was more in respect to reading books of literature, — well written standard works by infidel or sceptical writers, or by authors who were not in the least degree Christians. Thee knows there are a great many of that kind, who have printed books which are beautifully written, and which every cultivated man should know about. What shall I do about these? Thee has only partially settled my perplexities.

"Do suggest some method of carrying on our little morning meeting, so as to make it lively and interesting."

I replied to this on the 14th of May:

"As to thy questions about reading, I would say, emphatically, No! to any reading *for amusement* which would have a tendency to draw off thy mind from the truth as it is in Jesus. Reading *for information* is another thing, as all information is valuable in one's Christian work; but as it is impossible to read everything, or to pursue all branches of literature, we ought, I think, to choose those which will help, and not hinder, our Christian life; and a man is far more intelligent who thoroughly masters one branch, than if he has a smattering of a great many. Read all the books that will really strengthen thy mind and do thee good; and then, if thee has any time left, thee can consider about reading other things. I think the Holy Spirit is the best guide, however; if He makes us feel uneasy with any reading, then we *must* give it up. My darling boy, let nothing stand in the way of entire abandonment to the Lord. Indeed, this is the only happy way to live, and it will not cut thee off from any pleasure which is really worth having, or which could make thy life brighter in any true sense.

"I cannot tell thee what a comfort and a joy thee is to me, nor how tenderly I love thee. My confidence in thee is perfect, my boy."

About the same time his father also wrote to him in reference to these subjects:

"LOUISVILLE, May 4, 1872.

"MY DARLING BOY:

"Weighing one hundred and fifty pounds, and being stronger than I am, leaves thee still *my* 'boy.'

"Thy letter is most welcome. I have been deeply impressed, in reading John Wesley's Life, by what he accomplished through definiteness of purpose, and steady, unwavering persistence in work. He was at his work, — always at it, — hard at it; and his life-work has, through God, told on the history of the human race. Could his life but convey this lesson to our 'boy,' whose life-long habits are now being formed, what might we not expect from his early start in the good path!

"And it is so sweet to know that, while we yield ourselves as 'instruments of righteousness,' we do not have to furnish the *power* for work. Our Heavenly Father does this; we only 'do not frustrate' His purposes, but just *let* Him work in us to will and to do. The effort is not that of 'doing,' but of allowing Him to do, unhindered by ourselves.

"Has thee noticed that the greatest instruments in God's hand have been *educated* men? — Moses, Daniel, Paul! What a motive for intense effort to grasp all thy privileges in this respect. Many of the most deeply spiritual men of our day have the highest education; and while thee forever gives up ambition in thy studies, the love of God should be the motive with thee, as selfish ambition is with others. *Surely*, this should be more all-controlling than ambition to a child of God. Ignorant Christians are not, therefore, spiritual, nor is it the tendency of ignorance to make them so. There are probably a hundred ignorant Christians to one educated one; but I question if the *proportion* of sluggish Christians is not far greater in the ranks of the ignorant. Of the stewardship of his natural faculties my son has to give an account, and his responsibility now is for a liberal cultivation and enlargement of them; — not for self, but for God.

"The unusual mercies which surround thee may waft thee on to untold blessings! God grant that they may not be used for self, or cause indolence, so that severe sorrow may become needful to prepare thee to receive real blessings!

"If some around thee are not in earnest, I trust that there is at least *one* who is taking Christ in His promises, and leading a quiet but 'real life hid with Christ in God'; and, from this Rest, boldly witnessing 'where his sanctified judgment shows it is best' for the Lord Jesus.

"Do not feel that I am *criticising*, — I *greatly* joy in my boy; so much that I want to see him a holy, outspoken witness for his Lord.

"Thy loving father,

"ROBERT PEARSALL SMITH."

CHAPTER XV.

TO his cousin M——, Frank wrote on May 11th from College:

"... . I am glad thy father set me right on that question, when I was with you, for my theory was just a sort of outgrowth of a rather puerile brain. However, the outgrowth cleared the way for the good plant, which will be much more firmly rooted for having its ground stirred up a little. I knew thy secret delight at seeing me 'squenched,' and really enjoyed it with thee. It is fun to have ideas though, even if they are erroneous; I am sick of getting everything second-hand.

"I would like to 'let off' to thee about what I ought to be doing at present, instead of idly dreaming about other more interesting things I might be doing. The first thing I want to do is to carry out that maxim, 'Know thyself,' and find out about my own mind and its workings. Well, it *is* fine here at college, where every one is studying, and where the general influence is brain-stimulating. But I long for a truly sympathizing, congenial friend like we are to each other. How grand it is that we shall be together next summer at 'the Cedars,' and can read together and talk.

"And now don't let us spend all our time dreaming of doing something grand, and allow the present to go; but let us earnestly regard the present, each moment as we have it, as a priceless treasure to be used, and not to be dreamed away. I do not mean to say a little dreaming now and then will hurt us for actual work; but I like what Longfellow says in his *Psalm of Life:*

> 'Act, act in the living present.'

Not act in some grand way in the future, but act now. I have no objection to having an ideal in moderation, but I cannot afford to let it carry me away from the duties of the 'living present.'

"Oh, I heard such a splendid speech, in our Hall, the other night; it was on 'Failure,' and the fellow said that a man who had honestly and truly tried some great object and had failed, was as worthy of praise as the one who succeeded; that but for those who had failed, none would ever succeed; and that many men become mere nothings in the world, because they do not dare to fail. Do let us dare to fail, if it is inevitable, and then perhaps some one else, out of our wrecked hopes, may build up a firm edifice. What difference who builds the great house of our objects, so that it is only built? And if we can be but the corner-stone, hidden away down in the foundation, we will know the building rests on us, and that, unless we had been so buried, the building could not have been built.

"I never had thought of thy illustration of the knight and his armor. We have always so admired those stories of our dear old heroes, Launcelot, and

Galahad, and Tristram, and the rest; and it is splendid to be able to think of them in connection with ourselves and our poor lives, which seem so unromantic. But just here comes a question which is to me one of extreme importance. The knights of all our dear old romances fought for some lady, and laid their trophies at her feet. Now who are we three knights to fight for, and at whose feet do we propose to lay our trophies? I don't want to lecture, and especially not to preach; but do we expect to give the glory of our lives to ourselves, or to God? He asks for it, and are we to keep it for ourselves? Oh! let us look at this fairly and squarely, and have no flinching to commence with. I am far more in earnest than ever before; and I do think this is the question to start with. We are not to lay our honors at God's feet in a general way, and really keep them ourselves; but personally and particularly He must have them all. Please, don't call this a 'preach,' for I am just putting down what is going on in my own mind on this subject.

"I do hope our lives, as thee says, may lie side by side, in the pursuit of our ideal. Our paths may be very different; but that we may each help and encourage the other, in our upward way, I do sincerely hope.

"Thee knows it is said, a man can make himself whatever he pleases; and thee also knows, probably, that I am naturally very careful of what people say. Now, without running to the other extreme, I want to go ahead and do what I ought to do, as if there was no 'Mrs. Grundy.' Maybe thee will help me a little, as it will be tough work fighting one's nature.

"But I must stop, and sign myself thy fellow-climber up the Ideal mountain; and though the way is rough, and there are many briers, and it perplexes us sometimes to know our path, still there is the top always above us, and here and there we see resting-places, and dreamlands, and we can help each other a little. So let us hope.

"Thy prosaic cousin, FRANK."

On the 19th he wrote to me, still continuing the question as to the proper sort of reading for a young Christian:

". . . . I am not quite settled on the reading point yet. Thee says not to read anything for amusement, which will draw my mind away from divine things; of course, I agree to that. But, when we read for instruction, ought we not to choose out those books which are written in the best style on the subjects we are studying? For instance, ought I to read Hume, when I am reading English History; or ought I to reject him, because he was an infidel? Ought I to refuse to read Gibbon's History of Rome for the same reason? Or, carry it a little further, ought I to read Livy or Homer, for they were Pagans?

"I am just beginning to realize how very crude my mind is; and, in fact, to think that I have never really thought before. I suspect I have been pretty full of emptiness for the last sixteen years or so, and am just waking up to the fact. It is very hard work to learn really to think. But I am trying to put my self through on metaphysics, and to follow out a very few ideas of my own.

"I am going to put another question to thee that puzzles me. How far is ambition right? I mean, am I to hold before myself a desire to do something great and good; or, should I rather expect to be just a commonplace humdrum sort of man, doing good of course as much as I can, but never making much effort or stir? I could not bear the thought of settling down into nothingness. Now, *is* it wrong to seek for influence and a name, using, of course, perfectly right means? I hope I have made myself clear, for I want the question answered, please.

"I do not know of anything I have not given up. I acknowledge I *would* feel a little disappointed, if I should be called to go as a missionary to the South Sea Islands, for instance; but still I would go. I could not, however, help the feeling of disappointment. But despite my consecration and trust, which are earnest, so far as I know, I do not feel that exquisite joy some speak of, except at very rare intervals, when thee, or father, or some one, stirs me up."

I replied to this letter as follows:

"That reading-question *is* a difficult one, I confess. I think I would not object to read a History written by an infidel, if it was a standard work; but I would not read any book by the same author, written on the subject of religion. Hume's *History* would not hurt; but his book on Miracles might be of untold injury to the soul. I think the only really safe and wise plan is to pray about thy reading, and to trust the Lord Himself to teach thee. Thee need not form any *plan,* but just take each book as it presents, to the Lord, and ask Him about it, and if thy heart feels free to read it, then do so; I think this will solve the difficulty.

"As to thy other question, I would answer, emphatically, that it is right for a Christian to try and be the very best he can. Paul says to Timothy, 'Study to show thyself approved, a workman that needeth not to be ashamed.' Our Master wants to have polished instruments for His service; and it is thy duty to use thy present training-time to the very best advantage. No, we must not settle down into anything humdrum or commonplace. Be in everything the best thee can. Get all the influence thee can, and all the power thee can, and consecrate it to the Lord. Don't let Satan have all the benefit of ambition in his kingdom; but let thy soul be fired with a holy ambition to excel in everything for the Lord's sake,—just as father prayed that his management of the factories at M. might be successful, in order that Christ might be glorified. The longing to be something and to do something is divinely implanted in every heart, and it would be unnatural to try and quench it; all we must do is, to let this longing reach out after doing and being something for the Lord; and this is glorious ambition! To be co-workers with God, how grand! What a destiny to be ours! To be made a partner of Rothschild would be something; but to be made a partner of God, how immeasurably more! Paul says, 'Covet earnestly the best gifts,' so it is our duty to do it.

"As for joy, dear Frank, do not be troubled at not having it continually. Our feelings vary with the variations in our physical condition, or our surroundings; but our faith may remain unchanged through everything, and it is this we must watch over. Our joy is very sweet to us, but our faith is more precious to the Lord."

To his father, Frank wrote, on the 22d of May:

". . . . This Princeton atmosphere is waking me up, intellectually, a good deal. I am beginning to realize, as I have not fully done before, that my mind needs a great deal of cultivation in every respect. I am storing up all the good practical sayings I hear; and am acting on them whenever I can. One thing I am trying very hard to persist in, and that is to be doing something all the time; never to idle, or trifle away time, as thee advised me. So don't think thy admonitions are altogether thrown away, even if I do not act immediately on them.

"Thee cannot realize for me the necessity of keeping myself pure, half as much as I realize it for myself—pure both in body and mind. It is, in fact, my most earnest prayer that I may be made entirely so.

"I want to know, father, if it is possible for us to give ourselves in an entire abandonment to Christ, unless we are brought to it by some trial? I don't think a person ought to wait for that trial; but, somehow, I seem to think that no one can know the *full* preciousness of 'abiding in Christ,' until they have some sorrow; and I am afraid I will not until then."

This was our boy's last letter to his home; and the question with which it closed was destined to be gloriously answered in the brightness of the Lord's presence, where he was so soon to enter upon the fulness of joy for evermore, with no need of sorrow or of discipline ever again. It was his blessed portion to yield the free-hearted consecration of a life that had never known any deep trial; and to be in his own sweet experience a happy proof that sorrow is not a necessary preparation for abiding in Christ, but only the alternative, where the tender wooings of grace have not proved effectual.

Frank's eyes failing him, as they usually did in the spring, he came home the last day of May, and was unable to complete the collegiate year. And before another College year rolled round, he had done with colleges forever, and had entered upon the life where all the treasures of wisdom and knowledge are opened to his eager spirit, and where the highest aspirations of his soul, after a full and perfect development, have been lost in amazed surprise at the infinity made his own.

After his return home, Frank had a very happy time, visiting his friends, and enjoying the quiet country pleasures at "the Cedars," where we had gone about the first of June.

Among other visits, he spent several days with some of the old Hestonville party at West Chester and Wilmington, and was delighted at this opportunity of renewing and strengthening the sweet ties of Christian friendship that had been formed two years before. Two of the party were engaged to be married, and this, of course, introduced an element of great interest to Frank, who laughed a good deal in his quiet, happy way, as he told me on his return of the fun he had in attempting to tease the youthful pair.

As always upon their reunion, so now, this precious band of young Christians found one of their sweetest sources of enjoyment, when together, to consist in their religious fellowship, and in the little occasional prayer-meetings they managed always to have. Frank himself did not say much about this to me; but one young lady of the party, writing to me since, says:

"Very much of our intercourse during those days at West Chester and Wilmington was religious, — and was very precious. The expression of Frank's face, as he testified during that time to the Lord's goodness to him, and especially the tones of his voice as they rose in earnest pleading to the throne of Grace, have come back to me over and over with wonderful power and reality.

"The last prayer-meeting we ever had together was at Westchester on First-day night. There were some young people there of whose Christian standing we did not feel sure, and when Frank was talking of having the meeting, he said: 'Now is the time to show our colors, and we must not be afraid to do it.'

"That meeting I shall never forget. Frank prayed; and although I cannot recall the words of his prayer, I remember realizing that he had grown very much since I had heard him pray before. He was very anxious for the conversion of one of his friends, and regretted very much that we had not had a little prayer-meeting together while this one had been with us. But at last, he said, we must leave it all with the Lord, since He had not seemed to make a way for the meeting, and must believe that He would make all things work for the best.

"When we left W., we rode in the cars together for two or three hours, and had a delightful talk on religious subjects. We spoke of the right sort of conversation for Christians, of the medium between austerity and too great freedom. He told me also of a conversation he had had with his father, which had been a great comfort and help to him, in which his father had said, that a young Christian need not be discouraged because he had not the depth of peace and rest he saw in those more advanced; for that these grew with our growth, and were always greater in those whose experience in this Higher Life had been of longer duration."

The only letter Frank wrote after this was one sent from "the Cedars," on the 19th of June, to his cousin Minnie, whom he was eagerly expecting to join him there:

"Dear Minnie:

"Could n't before. Dreadful sorry. Sore eyes. Came home; been visiting ever since. . . . .

"Feel prepared for our work this summer, which is to be our armor-making time? We can blow each other's fires, only I am afraid mine has the least fuel, and will burn out the quickest. The Philadelphia

Library will not be shut up, so we can have that all summer. Does thee know yet what books we want?

"Do hurry on here, so that we can talk. I think abstract subjects afford an endless field of fun to us. We have hardly ever thought about them before, and they have the charm of being fresh. It is a perfect joy to me to talk about them, so do hurry on to 'the Cedars.'

"Do let us put a little practical into our dreams. First, if thee and I are to accomplish anything, how can we do it best, — by writing, by public speaking, or by our individual influence over individuals? Second, where can we do it best? And, third, what, when done, will amount to most; that is, will do others most good? We must talk this over this summer, and then set to work definitely to prepare ourselves; just as Herodotus worked at his style that he might write a history, or as Demosthenes overcame his stammering that he might become an orator. Hard work and steady application to one purpose will accomplish wonders; and as I need wonders, I must have the hard work and application. I am willing to put years of hard work on my 'ideal,' and then fail, if necessary; though I most certainly shall not fail, if hard work can help it.

". . . . We do need a great deal of armor, and so, it seems to me, we should direct our especial and earnest attention to finding out what weapons we really must have, in order that we may get only such as will be most useful; not attempting any which there is but little probability of our ever using. We must read as much as our eyes and health will permit; exercise as much of the remaining time as we can; find out things by talking whenever and wherever we get a chance; and, while we are exercising, and all the rest of the time, think! It is an intensely interesting occupation to me, to find out the best way to think. No one can tell another; each one must find it out for himself. Another thing, we must study human nature.

"Much obliged for what thee said about the reality of my consecration. I do want it to be real."

On the 1st of July the large party of cousins gathered at "the Cedars," all bright with health and spirits, little thinking that, before two short months would pass, the oldest of that happy group would be taken from their midst, to join the company of the redeemed in Heaven.

On the 4th of July, Frank joined us at Sea Cliff Grove, on Long Island, where we had gone a few days previously, to attend the National Camp Meeting for the promotion of Holiness, or "the Higher Christian Life." For ten days we camped out there in tents, attending meetings having this definite subject in view all day long. Our dear boy enjoyed the services of these ten days exceedingly, and felt it to have been a season of great blessing to his soul. A young lady, with whom he was much associated during these meetings, thus writes concerning him:

"During these pleasant ten days I spent with Frank, I had many conversations with him on religious subjects, in which he helped me to come out decidedly on the Lord's side; especially he helped me to understand the subject of sanctification by faith; and, although he never said much about himself, still I knew from his conversation that he enjoyed this blessing. I found a friend in him such as I have never found in any other young man.

"In one of our 'young people's meetings,' he spoke of the trials and temptations of College life, and of his own weakness; but told us of his confidence in God's power to deliver him and strengthen him. He also spoke in one of the more public meetings, confessing his entire consecration to the Lord, and his sweet sense of being fully accepted by Him."

Another lady, older than himself, who was much with him while there, says:

"I shall not soon forget some of the sweet talks I had with Frank at Sea Cliff about the Higher Life. In one of these he said, 'I think the best way is to *live* Christ, and then, when we speak, we will be believed;' and added, that he did pray that his life in College might be such as would make his fellow-students believe holiness to be attainable. He said, on another occasion, that he thought it did not do much good to argue about this doctrine, but to let people understand plainly your own faith in regard to it, as if you were not ashamed of it, and then hold on to it firmly, without getting angry at anything they might say or do; he said he thought 'this had more influence than anything else.'

"In the last conversation we had together, he said, after speaking of his responsibilities because of so much teaching; 'But I do not think much about the future. I do not know why it is, but somehow I cannot make any plans for the coming College year; I do not look that far into the future. I never before felt just as I do now; but I know the Lord will lead me, and I just leave it with Him. I want to work for Christ; but I only want to do it in whatever way He may see best.'

"In reply I quoted those lines:

> "'It may not be my way; it may not be thy way;
> But yet, in His own way, the Lord will provide.'

Adding, 'and we need not arrange nor choose.' I seem now to see his smile and the bright light in his eye, as he answered, 'Yes, the Lord's way *is* best for us all.'

"Ah! little did we know that even then the path of glory was the Lord's way for him; and that a few more days would reveal to his enraptured gaze the gates of the celestial city!

"How often have his words, with their sweet emphasis, recurred to me since, when tempted to question or complain — 'The Lord's way *is* best;' and they have many times strengthened faith and love in my soul."

Our dear boy returned from Sea Cliff to "the Cedars" on the 15th of July, and spent a happy week with his cousins there, in all sorts of out-door amusements, and in the "armor-making" work they had been so long planning.

On the 22d of July, 1872, the four older cousins, Frank, M., B., and W., started on a long anticipated "expedition," to explore the upper stream of the Brandywine. The company consisted of half a dozen of the Hestonville party, and a few more of their young friends, and it was led by the father of two of the young ladies. They met at his summer home near West Chester, Pa.; and taking several carriages, and a wagon with provisions for pic-nicking, they drove leisurely through the beautiful scenery of Chester, Lancaster, and Berks counties, lodging at night at the village inns, and stopping by day to explore, and climb, and row, as their fancy dictated. From the wooded heights of Ephrata they looked over a broad expanse comprising many of the eastern counties of Pennsylvania; and returning by way of Coatesville, had an unsurpassed view of the "Great Valley," from Caln meeting-house, after a charming ramble along the West Branch of the Brandywine. Each member of the party had an office. Frank was "Botanist;" and the very names, "Historian," "Astronomer," "Artist," "Poet," "Hostler," "Caterer," and "Picker-up," will long recall to all of them vivid scenes of adventure, some full of fun, others of serious danger.

The friend from whose house they started writes as follows, concerning this short episode in our boy's life:

"While I had known Frank from a little child, my acquaintance with him had been but slight before our living together during these pleasant days. I cannot well put into words the sense that grew upon me of the remarkable combination of manliness and meekness in his character. There was a magnetism about him that brought one very close to him. Before the beginning of each day's fun and work, and after it was over, we drew near together to the same Mercy-seat, and at such times his soul seemed to take hold of the Invisible with an earnestness rare in one so young. The Lord Jesus was with him an ever present Friend and Helper; so that, whether in the height of our enjoyment, or in the more serious moments when we talked together of the ways of God, he was alike a faithful witness for Him whom he loved. What I now recall most vividly, as I look back to this little journey, is the modesty and ingenuousness he exhibited in all our undertakings, the unselfishness he constantly showed when it was not easy to prefer others to himself, and the fact, very early apparent, that he was to be absolutely trusted in any duty assigned him.

"He was not very well on two or three occasions, and more than once he expressed what now seems a strange presentiment of his early death. One of the party relates that, as they stood together in a little country graveyard, Frank said to her, 'I wonder which of us will be taken first? I think I shall die young!' And, after the return of the party to West Chester, the evening before they separated, as they sat in the moonlight on the piazza, the conversation turned again, as it often had, upon death and the wonders to be revealed to us hereafter. Frank did not take an active part in this, but was silent and thoughtful. But at another time when we were together, as if in unconscious recognition of the change so soon to come to him, he called attention to the closing passages in Tennyson's *Morte D'Arthur,* and repeated aloud the impressive lines beginning:

> 'Ah, my Lord Arthur! whither shall I go?'
> . . . .
> And slowly answered Arthur from the barge:
> 'The old order changeth, yielding place to new
> And God fulfils Himself in many ways,
> Lest one poor custom should corrupt the world.
> Comfort thyself! What comfort is in me?
> *I have lived my life, and that which I have done*
> *May He Himself make pure!* But thou
> If thou shouldst never see my face again,
> Pray for my soul. More things are wrought by prayer
> Than this world dreams of.
> . . . .
> But now, farewell! I am going a long way
> To the island valley of Avilion;
> Where falls not hail, or rain, or any snow,
> Nor ever wind blows loudly; but it lies
> Deep-meadowed, happy, fair with orchard lawns,
> And bowery hollows crowned with summer sea,
> Where I will heal me of my grievous wound.'

"Some of us who heard him can never read these words again without associating them with our last hours with Frank on earth."

The night after the return of our four to "the Cedars," we had our usual First-day evening Bible class in grandpa Whitall's parlor. The subject of our lesson was the "Present possessions of the believer;" and dear Frank was very much interested. When the text, "He that believeth hath everlasting life," was read, a very earnest discussion followed, in which he seemed to be seeking to enter into the meaning of these wonderful words more deeply than ever he had done before, as though his soul might have felt the foreshadowing of the glorious unfolding of this life, which a few short days was to bring him. We talked until pretty late, and the last words dear Frank said, as I kissed him good-night in the hall, were something in reference to this eternal life. Had I but known that never again would I have an opportunity of talking with my son on these blessed themes, how much there was I would have said and asked! And yet there was no need; for, surely, never had there been a sweeter or fuller intimacy between parents and child, than had always existed between our son and ourselves.

The next day was his last well day on earth, the last opportunity he and his cousin M—— ever had for their "armor-making." They climbed into a favorite tree, and read to each other out of Dante and Milton; and learned together a little poem, which seems now strangely significant of the parting that was so soon to come:

> "I go my way, thou goest thine,
> Many ways we wend;
> Many days and many ways
> Ending in one end.
> Many a wrong and its curing song,
> Many a road and many an inn;
> Room to roam, but only one Home
> For the whole world to win."

And Frank's last words to this darling cousin were these lines, so prophetic, which he repeated to her that night as they separated on the stairs on their way to bed.

The next day Frank seemed drooping. We attributed it to the fatigue of the expedition at first; but a bad headache coming on, and continuing, we put him to bed, and sent for the doctor. His grandma Whitall arranged a chamber for him in the quiet of their larger house, just across the lawn from our little cottage; and there, surrounded by all the tender care that love could give, he passed the ten days of his illness, and closed his eyes on earth in the very spot of all others that he and we would have chosen, could we have arranged it for ourselves.

The first day of his sickness the thought passed through my mind that it might be typhoid fever; and as I sat beside his bed with my work, an instinct within me seemed to urge me to ask him for some last words of assurance and peace, although I little thought they would be the last. I said to him, "Frank, this may be typhoid fever. Suppose it is, would thee be afraid to die?" "Oh, no," he answered, very cheerfully, "not at all." We sat silent for a few moments after this, while I was pursuing in my own mind the thoughts of the blessedness of being taken home to Heaven, and how greatly it was to be desired by all of us; and then I continued, "It would be rather nice, after all, to die, — would n't it, Frank?" "Why, yes," was his still cheerful reply, "it would. *Only I would like to live and work for Jesus.*" I comforted him with saying that he need not trouble himself about this; that, if the Lord wanted him He would keep him, and if He did not, it would be glorious to enter so early upon the unspeakable bliss of being with Jesus. And this was the last talk I ever had with my boy!

He rapidly grew worse, became delirious, and was so very sick that it seemed unkind to rouse him, even to answer a question. On the fifth day of his illness, his father was sitting beside him, and, in a lucid moment, he turned and said, "Father, is this the end?" "I think not," was his father's reply; "but if it should be, it will all be well." "Oh, yes," he exclaimed, "I know that, but then I would have liked to have done some work for *Him!*" In a moment he was wandering again, and these were his last intelligent words.

On the afternoon of the 8th he had a struggle which lasted for a short time, and then he gradually but surely failed. The cold chill of death slowly crept up his limbs, his breath grew shorter and shorter, and at half-past five o'clock, on the afternoon of the 8th of August, 1872, Frank's earthly life was over, and his glorious heavenly life with Jesus had begun.

Our son had left us. But the sweet memories of his life, and the precious savor of his dedicated spirit were with us still; and every relic we found among his papers and his private treasures, only revealed to us afresh how deep and true had been his Christian experience. The next day after his death we took from the pocket of his every-day coat, which we found hanging in his room, his little daily note-book, and there we met with a sweet surprise; for we found his last precious confession, in the form of the consecration on the opposite page, which reveals in its completeness the secret of his pure and happy life.

Another precious consolation awaited us when we opened the Bible which had been Frank's constant companion ever since his fourteenth birthday, in 1868. We found it full of pencil-marks made around his favorite verses, — revealing, in this way, much of his inner life, and his appreciation of the truth of God. Especially we rejoiced to see that those verses which declare the love and goodness of God, and develop the simplicity of a life of faith in the Lord Jesus Christ, were the most deeply marked; and that the last chapters in Revelation, where the glories and the joys of Heaven are revealed, had also been peculiarly precious to him, while as yet he had had no thought of so soon entering into the possession of them.

> "Some gentle souls there are who yield unto my love,
> And ripening fast beneath my care, I early can remove."

Such was our boy. All that many an older Christian has learned only through years of painful discipline and sore trials, his fresh young heart apprehended by a childlike faith, while yet his life was free from care or sorrow, and filled with all its early brightness.

The Gospel had come to him as, in very truth, "glad tidings of great joy;" he had believed it, and it had made him happy. And it was no half-gospel he believed, nor was it a partial Saviour in whom he trusted, but Jesus was to him a full, a perfect, and a present Saviour from the power, as well as from the guilt of sin; and his life bore daily and hourly witness to the reality of his trust, and to the mighty power and perfect trustworthiness of his Saviour.

It was Frank's singular privilege to learn in the beginning of his Christian life the Way of Faith. Not only was the truth that we are justified by faith, and made the children of God by faith, understood by him, but he also apprehended the far deeper truth, that the believer is called to live by faith, to stand by faith, to walk by faith, and to overcome by faith; and it is no wonder, that, possessing this secret, his soul early ripened for Heaven, and the Lord could call him home.

On his eighteenth birthday, the 12th of August, 1872, he was committed to the earth in Laurel Hill Cemetery, in the sure hope of a joyous resurrection.

A DEDICATION.

I take God the Father to be my God.
1 THESS. 1: 9.

I take God the Son to be my Saviour.
ACTS 5: 31.

I take God the Holy Ghost to be my Sanctifier.
1 PETER 1: 2.

I take the Word of God to be my rule.
2 TIM. 3: 16, 17.

I take the people of God to be my people.
RUTH 1: 16, 17.

I likewise dedicate my whole self to the Lord.
ROM. 14: 7, 8.

And I do this deliberately.
JOSH. 24: 15.

Sincerely.
2 COR. 1: 12.

Freely.
PSA. 110: 3.

And for ever.
ROM. 8: 35, 39.

www.ingramcontent.com/pod-product-compliance
Lightning Source LLC
LaVergne TN
LVHW011213110826
845150LV00006B/1419

* 9 7 8 1 4 2 5 5 1 7 5 8 8 *